BUSINESS SUCCESS

THROUGH SELF-KNOWLEDGE

WILLIAM D. ANTON, PhD

*Business leaders who are committed to broadening access
to their own potential through increasing their self-knowledge
are in the very best position to improve the quality and level of
performance within their organization.*

Published by CEOEFFECTIVENESS, LLC
15961 North Florida Avenue, Suite A
Lutz, Florida 33549

ISBN 978-0-615-731-33-9

Printed in the USA

This book is designed for business leaders who are no longer satisfied with relative success and have become curious about the unexplored territory within themselves, where untapped potential patiently waits; and for professional consultants who understand the importance of their position as leaders of the transformation process and providers of opportunity for organizational leaders to align with the path that others in their company are encouraged to take.

"'The brain is malleable throughout life.' With his opening sentence, Dr. Anton says it all, and he gives everyone hope. Each of us has the opportunity throughout life to learn information and skills that can improve how our brain actually works. But what to learn? Dr. Anton effectively argues that self-knowledge is priority one. He's right. As a psychologist over the past 40 years, I have had the opportunity to observe people in all walks of life, including leaders of famous organizations. Those who develop self-knowledge gain a dramatic advantage. Leaders who graduate from self-imposed small circles of self-knowledge to larger circles access potential within themselves that widens success and enables them to lead others to higher performance. Want people in your organization to be self-aware? Set the example! Dr. Anton has provided a fast-start guide. You won't be sorry that you read it. You'll be thrilled if you act on it."

Dana C. Ackley, PhD
Executive coach and consultant
President, EQ Leader, Inc.
Author, *Breaking Free of Managed Care:*
A Step-by-Step Guide to Regaining Control of Your Practice

"Dr. Anton's *Business Success Through Self-Knowledge* is an extraordinarily clear, easy-to-read, well-documented, and intelligently written book. It will prove to be of enormous practical value to CEOs and to anyone appointed to positions of leadership, at any level and in any area, including chairmen or chairwomen of all kinds in university departments and non-profit organizations, professionals, and even politicians. As he rightly points out, a look inside themselves, with the consequent acquisition of self-knowledge, by those at the top significantly improves their abilities to use empathy, skills, and expertise. Similarly, he points out a most rewarding way to improve the functioning, success, effectiveness, and health of organizations and their members. I highly recommend this book to practically anyone living in this time and age."

Humberto Nágera, MD
Director, the Carter-Jenkins Center
Professor emeritus of psychiatry,
University of Michigan and University of South Florida
Author, *Obsessional Neuroses: Developmental Psychopathology*
and *Childhood Psychopathology: A Developmental Approach*

"Socrates stated that 'the unexamined life is not worth living' but did not provide the framework for understanding how to obtain self-knowledge. Lucky for us, Dr. Anton has provided a helpful and insightful road map for understanding ourselves and others. Few books offer such a clear path for how we can tap our potential, increase our focus, and feel engaged. *Business Success Through Self-Knowledge* is a must-read for executives and mentors."

Dr. Mary Lippitt
Author, *The Leadership Spectrum*
Coauthor, *Discover Your Inner Strengths*

"A powerful new book on the human nature of business success, *Business Success Through Self-Knowledge* provides a compelling and practical lens into the real frontier, which is not only ahead of us but also inside us. In order to grow yourself and your business, you must better know yourself. In a world flooded with business books that mostly miss the mark, this one stands apart and shines. Dr. Anton is a deeply experienced and wise counselor to top executives: This is a must-read for leaders and professionals at every level and in every field!"

Robert K. Cooper, PhD
CEO of Cooper Strategic
Founder of 12 Leaders
Best-selling author, *The Other 90%* and *Get Out of Your Own Way*

"This is a seminal work that should create a wide ripple throughout the business community and beyond. Dr. Anton has tapped into something that's fundamental to almost every aspect of business, not to mention human, life. One of the profound insights of the work is that—contravening popular belief—human nature is not unchangeable and static but is subject to development. Yet the process is not automatic. On the contrary, development takes a pathway, and this important work shows the way forward. The path to greater strength, first for the individual and then for the organization, lies in favorably resolving the self-negotiation we all face between retreating into the comfort zone of our self-imposed limitations and the far more challenging, yet rewarding, task of actively striving to grasp the untapped potential that lies dormant in us all."

Frank Mobus
Executive vice president, Karrass

"This book is a must-read for anyone leading two, tens, or hundreds of people. Dr. Anton shows how leaders can become vastly more competitive by embracing the often elusive personal mastery so many of us seek."

Jaynie L. Smith
Author, *Creating Competitive Advantage* and *Relevant Selling*

"Why is acquiring self-knowledge so critical for businesses that want to be exceptional? In this exciting new work, Dr. Anton clearly demonstrates the importance of leadership self-knowledge as a business strategy and in creating a competitive advantage. In doing so, he integrates information and ideas from great thought leaders along with the wisdom and knowledge he has personally gained from working with organizational leaders for more than 30 years. He also includes essential ideas and resources and identifies the next steps for leaders who are committed to their own personal mastery and that of their organization. The rewards are great for those who read this book and take the journey to greater self-knowledge and self-discovery—especially leaders at the top of any organization."

R. Bob Smith III, PhD
Chairman and CEO, PAR, Inc.

Contents

Acknowledgements

This book is dedicated to evolving the capacity of organizations and individuals to create purposeful futures. It is an extension of my work as a psychologist, psychoanalyst, and executive coach and is focused on the group of leaders who sense their unrealized potential but have not yet reached the threshold that compels them to take purposeful action.

This book was also developed for consultants who seek to recapture more of their own unrealized potential by first applying the transformational learning they seek for others to themselves.

All the themes in this book can be expanded with additional information and documentation. My academic and scientific sides struggled in the pursuit of keeping the book brief and practical given the subject matter and the audience for which it was intended.

My life's foundation is anchored in three people, and I am filled with gratitude for them: my parents, Willie and Lydia Anton, who lived lives characterized by confidence, unselfishness, belief in God, absence of malice, thirst for learning, and commitment to doing good and helping others; and my aunt Jessie Anton Mitchell, a school principal who gave generously to others and was universally loved by all who knew her. By believing in my potential, these three loving people taught me the importance of nourishing my soul by offering my best to others.

Many other family, friends, colleagues, and clients contributed in various ways that helped me explore the relationship between self-knowledge and leadership effectiveness from different vantage points, and I am thankful for them. Some are mentioned here specifically for their willingness to offer their time, ideas, and suggestions to this work.

I am grateful for the help graciously provided by my wife Jean, a psychotherapist in her own right, for offering her perspectives and editorial suggestions throughout the process of writing this book. I am also grateful to my son, Dr. Steve Anton, and my daughter, Christina Anton Garcia, Esq., who generously took time from their own demanding professional lives to offer edits, suggestions, and perspectives on language and images.

During the writing of this book, my sister Glenda Anton Midili, another school principal—who is always reading a new book—offered to read the manuscript on more than one occasion and each time made valuable suggestions that were helpful in improving the content narrative.

Although I have read hundreds of books on business, leadership, and organizations, the ideas expressed by five authors stand out in my mind as "on to something really important," and their works inspired me to write this book. They are Robert K. Cooper, Peter Senge, Margaret Wheatley, David Whyte, and J. Rufus Fears. I am especially grateful to Dr. Cooper for generously offering his guidance about the need for brief, well-researched practical books that communicate ideas and actions clearly and concisely.

I am grateful to Ron Fleisher, whose experience working with CEOs was invaluable in keeping my focus on the importance of alignment and the business advantages of leadership self-knowledge.

To my longtime colleague and friend Dr. R. Bob Smith, III, a psychologist and CEO and founder of Psychological Assessment Resources, I offer my thanks for his support and for lending his considerable experience in guiding the final product toward publication.

For the help it takes to transform a manuscript into a book I thank Nancy Howe for her expert work with the early phases of the project and for her many valued suggestions. I owe a great deal to Erika Thompson for her incredible copyediting skills and willingness to offer her valued ideas about so many important issues related to the book. I also owe a great deal to Sean Carey of HD Interactive for the development of CEOeffectiveness.com and for coordinating the brainstorming group mentioned next, and to James Silvera, illustrator extraordinaire, for his work with the Web site, book cover, and illustrations. Special thanks go to Dawn Pittaro, who designed the layout of the book's interior and typeset it with incredible attention to detail, and to

Mark Wallner, who was extremely helpful in coordinating the printing of the book.

I am grateful to Sean Davis, Marvin Scaff, and most especially John Morrow for their help in translating my ideas about elevating the purpose of business through leadership self-knowledge into a business-focused project and, ultimately, this book. John, an accomplished business owner, technology consultant, and avid reader, was supportive from the beginning and even agreed to write book reviews for my Web site, which he has done superbly.

There are others whom I also want to thank for their willingness to read all or parts of the early manuscripts and for offering their ideas and encouragement throughout the process. Some who have influenced my thinking in helpful ways include Dr. Dana Ackley, Dr. Mary Lippitt, Frank Mobus, and Jaynie Smith, all of whom are major authors or contributors to cutting-edge ideas in business consultation and negotiation. I also thank Dr. Hector Gonzalez, Jane Jenkins, and Frances Marton for reading early versions of the manuscript and offering helpful suggestions for improving my connection to the reader. I have the greatest respect for all of them.

Many others have offered encouragement, thoughtful perspectives, insights, support, and their vision of a better world. My colleagues on the executive board of the Tampa Bay Business Transition Council, Dan Maloney, John Morrow, Stratton Smith, Esq., and Michael Valdez, have all taught me a great deal. I am also grateful to the members of the council—in particular, Denise Clemence, Cindy Hesterman, John Hindman, and Linda O'Rourke—who have stimulated my thinking in ways that have helped me to clarify where my own contributions can be made more meaningful.

And to those persons who believe in their hearts that their future contributions will be greater than those of their past, I salute and encourage them to move forward with calm energy and confidence.

William D. Anton
Tampa, Florida
December 2012

Self-Knowledge:
The Master Key for Business and Life

The brain is malleable throughout life. How well we use it depends on knowing how our mind works. We are wired to connect on a social basis. Our brains are equipped with mirror neurons that can read the emotional subtext in every human interaction. They operate outside of consciousness but have an active influence on what we experience. We are always communicating, even when we're silent.

This book presents a path to gaining self-knowledge. After many years of working with leaders in industry and education, I have concluded that self-knowledge is the best business strategy. The path that I identify can apply to any business or service and is particularly critical, if not indispensable, for businesses today. They are faced with instant communications, emerging expectations from internal and external customers, and the ability of all customers to immediately expose and propagate their experiences with the organization. Self-knowledge can be the key to seamlessly negotiating issues that may not have been anticipated yet demand timely action. Self-knowledge is a prerequisite to greatness. And great organizations that are built from leadership self-knowledge and wisdom are not easily copied.

This book is intentionally brief and presents the basics for helping leaders gain greater access to their unrealized potential. It is not intended to be a substitute for working with a business or psychological consultant or coach. Nor does it purport to be an exhaustive review of the scientific research in the areas covered within. However, it presents essential knowledge that must be had by those who wish to approach their fuller potential and enhance their effectiveness as business leaders and people.

Preface

This above all: to thine own self be true,
And it must follow, as the night the day,
Thou canst not then be false to any man.

In these lines from Shakespeare's *Hamlet*, the flawed Polonius prepares his son for his travel abroad with a last piece of advice. Polonius is saying that intemperate pursuits are a way of being false to your real self. In fact, they are an indication that your life is filled with diversion and lack of focus. But you can only be true to yourself if you know your real self. This is not only knowing who you are at the moment, but also knowing why you behave, act, speak, and react the way you do. This level of understanding is the gateway to discovering and recapturing your missing parts, which have been patiently waiting in your subconscious. It is the meaning of becoming whole. As the process of self-knowledge evolves in your life, everything changes. You'll begin to see more clearly, view others more objectively, understand your reactions, and ultimately reduce the gap between your innate capacity and your actual, daily functioning. In short, you'll have greater access to your potential than you could have imagined.

Leadership self-knowledge is the *best* business strategy, particularly for those at the top levels of leadership.
This brief book is designed to focus on an indispensable but usually ignored technique for improving the health and effectiveness of organizations: the acquiring of CEO self-knowledge. How does self-knowledge fit into the final recipe for creating competitive advantage? This book will explain why self-knowledge is fundamental for the most effective application of knowledge, skills, talents, and abilities. It will show why it is so difficult to see and experience ourselves objectively and how we can begin to learn how our minds work.

But first, let's incorporate one of Steven Covey's seven habits of highly effective people (1989) and take a peek into the future: *let's begin with the end in mind.* If self-knowledge is the base, what are some other ingredients that are necessary for success? And how will these contribute to the success of the organization? Here is the basic equation:

$$\text{Leadership self-knowledge} + \text{shared vision} + \text{cultural alignment} = \text{Competitive advantage (i.e., success)}.$$

Shared vision represents something that everyone within the organization has collectively created. It's a purpose worthy of belief, a tenet or ideal that all employees aspire to achieve and can pursue whole-heartedly. *Cultural alignment* is the principle of considering the best interests of the customer, the company, and the employee—collectively, the *constituents*—and ensuring that the three are aligned. *Competitive advantage*, as used here, is creating and sustaining superior performance so that the constituents would choose your company or its products and services over the competition.

Most business writers would agree that top leadership self-knowledge is important for creating and nurturing healthy organizations and maintaining competitive advantage. In practice, however, the majority build models based on certain ingredients for achieving business success and organizational health and hope or assume that organizational leaders are emotionally and financially able to support their implementation. The reality is often quite different. Changes are implemented for a period of time and met with some initial success, but conditions are allowed to fade to previous levels before the changes are ever fully executed. This erosion is often blamed on the models themselves—or sometimes on the business consultants, who have offered important ideas that have been proven to work "in the lab" but are not viable in real-world business settings.

This all-too-familiar scenario is often a consequence of a common omission in business consulting. The transformation of the person at the top is not addressed in the model. And no amount of beneficial change is likely to take hold if the changes take place outside the comfort zone (i.e., level of self-awareness) of the person heading the enterprise. Acknowledging that the person in charge is crucial to organizational effectiveness, and that he or she should be committed and involved, is simply not enough to transform a struggling organization into a healthy one. Most people at the top are intelligent, knowledgeable, committed, and involved, but how these attributes are used is a function of how well each person knows him- or herself.

Perhaps an example outside of business will help to clarify this point. We all know families whose parents work hard to provide for their children, care very much about them and their happiness, and are committed to their success in life. They may even be well-educated, knowledgeable, and up-to-date on the best child-rearing practices. Yet, we can still identify subtle ways that caring parents can undermine important areas of their children's resiliency and success, particularly when we look closely at families with children whose development is grossly uneven. This is almost never intentional—it's rarely even conscious—but it can be evident to friends and relatives who view the family from unique vantage points. We sense that it takes more than good intentions and knowledge to raise a healthy child. The application of the knowledge is even more important than the knowledge itself. And we can apply our knowledge base effectively only when our level of self-awareness permits us to see our actions clearly and understand what needs to be done. I am reminded of a paradoxical quote by Oscar Wilde that relates to this point: "A gentleman is one who never hurts anyone's feelings unintentionally." What a beautiful way of expressing the relationship between responsibility and self-knowledge!

When well-intentioned efforts are made to offer advice to the parent or bring unacknowledged tendencies to his or her consciousness, the reaction can range from gratitude to anger. A grateful response will usually lead to an attempt to change, but gradually good intentions give way to embedded habits, which have had many more years of rehearsal and hence are much stronger. When the response is outright anger, successful change is even less likely. Only people who become curious about themselves can positively change their level of awareness. Because I have worked for many years with people who voluntarily seek to improve their effectiveness, I can say: It is extremely challenging for most people to see how they get in their own way, and it's even harder for them to acknowledge the parts of themselves they would prefer not to know. Information alone does not seem to have a great effect on personal change, especially when it comes from the outside.

You can't change organizations without changing the people within.
So why is this important for business leaders? It is only important if they want

to create real and sustainable change in organizations composed of people. And you'll gain the greatest leverage by starting with change at the top.

Years ago, many child therapists worked exclusively with children, creating during sessions a context that mirrored important elements of the home environment to help children gain greater control of their disruptive emotions. The children improved during the sessions but appeared to regress by the time of their next visit. We now realize that there is little benefit in working with the child if you don't work with the parents as well. All elements are important: parent, child, and context. But parents are in the best position to influence the context, and the context exerts a kind of gravity that influences and sustains change.

It isn't too much of a stretch to see how this applies to organizations. All elements and constituencies in an organization are important, but the point of optimal leverage is at the very top. If the person at the top has not invested the time required to know him- or herself, then it is unlikely that he or she will discover or embrace any paradigm that could liberate creative energy throughout the enterprise. The leader can't value what he or she cannot see.

So, if I could work with only one person in an organization, it would be the person at the top. And my focus would be on his or her personal mastery and awareness of his or her own mental models. He or she is in the best position to influence the context. The more clearly the leader sees how he or she contributes to what he or she experiences from others, the more effective will be any effort to improve the health and effectiveness of the organization.

If the executive at the top focuses outside of him- or herself to achieve corporate visions and goals without first objectifying what he or she knows about him- or herself, he or she may experience some success. But executives who do this rarely come close to what is possible. Being able to see how we get in our own way and actually plant self-limiting seeds along the way requires a unique kind of courage. Personal mastery that transforms neurobiology is not easily achieved and often impossible to accomplish through introspection alone. It requires knowing how our mind works from a more objective perspective. All who attempt this do not succeed, but there is no greater goal than transforming ourselves into self-aware beings.

Developing ourselves this way helps us use our energy in positive and purposeful ways. Our brain is designed to function as an integrated whole, and our bodies, thoughts, emotions, and relationships are the gauges that tell us how well our body-mind connection is working. Intellectual understanding and emotional intelligence can be developed—in fact, both are necessary if we are to become effective leaders who inspire others to become leaders themselves in the service of shared values and goals. Just like prudent investments, leadership self-knowledge compounds over time. It is the best platform for seeing clearly what needs to be done and how to accomplish these tasks through the constituents.

The purpose of this book is to provide busy executives a short path that can lead to enhanced self-knowledge and effectiveness. In essence, it deals primarily with the first of a three-part process: knowledge, understanding, and self-discovery. The perspectives presented herein represent the culmination of my many years of training and application in psychology, psychoanalysis, and upper-level leadership in large organizations. It integrates knowledge from psychology, business, and neuroscience in a concise manner that identifies what you need to know to begin the journey toward understanding and self-discovery.

This knowledge base is, in part, what I have used in working with businesses and business leaders in complex organizational frameworks. Experience in upper-level leadership in a large urban university and work with top-level CEOs have provided me a laboratory for applying, evaluating, and enhancing this knowledge base over the past two decades. More recently, I have worked as an executive coach to CEOs in both public and private corporations. As a result, my experience base includes knowledge of many real-life situations that executives face on a regular basis.

Business Success Through Self-Knowledge is composed of brief, concentrated sections designed to help you develop a framework for improving leadership effectiveness through personal mastery by seeing the big picture of your own life. Sections focus on what you need to know and how you can discover your path to greater sustainable personal and professional success. The level of success you can achieve may far exceed your expectations for you and your company. A lot of the potential energy and creativity crucial to business effectiveness is never tapped. You can learn to free and direct this creative energy within your organization by liberating your potential to create an innovative culture.

Before you begin, it is important to remember that the most powerful liberator of creativity, energy, and innovation in a business organization is leadership self-knowledge. Why?

- Leaders operate more objectively when they know how their own minds work. They can learn how to more carefully consider taking action that could result in mistakes or less effective decisions.

- Personal mastery is encouraged by directing the powerful variable of modeling throughout the organization.

- People emulating personal growth through self-knowledge are more genuinely committed to the organization and demonstrate improved job mastery by applying their talents and skills to their work.

- Leadership self-knowledge increases the likelihood of improved negotiations within the organization.

- An energized culture creates an atmosphere that greatly contributes to enhanced creativity and productivity.

- Relationships with your customers are greatly improved. Organizations with a heightened atmosphere of motivation and self-respect tend to pass that attitude on, all the way to the customer.

- And last, but certainly not least, your organization's competitive edge, a direct result of the leadership's commitment to self-knowledge, becomes a true advantage that is very difficult for others to copy. Because self-knowledge is dynamic (i.e., always changing as you continue to gain new insights), your competitive edge gets bigger as your self-knowledge grows. As others try to catch up with your organization, they will be puzzled at the seamless alignment of your constituents—while you and your team are already working on tomorrow's results!

When historical wisdom is supported by science, confidence is sustained by cross-validation in the short run and by measurable outcomes in the long run.

The following sections integrate ideas from distinguished researchers and leading business experts who have successfully demonstrated the tangible value of self-knowledge in creating great enterprises. The ideas presented represent the application and integration of historical wisdom, neuroscience findings, and psychological principles that have been shown to optimize business and organizational effectiveness.

Stimulating Excellence: Who Will They Emulate?

Sustaining competitive advantage by creating consistently high performance levels in others is a great challenge. The very best way to accomplish this is to win others' hearts. To engender that level of commitment, the business leader must be on the same path that he or she wants others to follow. This is the true currency for generating passion, commitment, and excellence in ourselves and others.

"A human being is a part of the whole, called by us 'Universe,' a part limited in time and space. He experiences himself, his thoughts and feelings as something separated from the rest—a kind of optical delusion of his consciousness. The striving to free oneself from this delusion is the one issue of true religion. Not to nourish the delusion but to try to overcome it is the way to reach the attainable measure of peace of mind."

                                                                Albert Einstein, 1950

This book has been incubating for a long time, perhaps since I was very young. When I was seven years old, I learned the value of moderation the hard way. After playing sports in the hot sun for the better part of a summer day in Florida, I arrived home with a headache. It was no ordinary headache. It was the first symptom of spinal meningitis, the bacterial kind. Playing too hard and too long without rest had run down my immune system and given invisible assailants an opportunity to gain the upper hand from their previously hidden home in my throat.

In many ways it was the end of my carefree days of excess and the beginning of my desire to understand the powerful forces that had changed my life. I was one of the fortunate few who did not die or suffer lifetime ill effects from this powerful assailant. Yet missing a year of school and being quite sick for many months (including a two-week stay at Johns Hopkins Hospital) gave me plenty of time to observe adults in various roles with a wide range of ability to connect with me and lift my spirits. Even as a young child it was apparent that the people who instilled hope in me seemed to be comfortable and happily engaged in their work. Years after my recovery, I realized that their kindness was based on a foundation of competence, inner peace, and knowing themselves enough to give freely without feeling depleted.

From working at a radio station beginning in eighth grade to my current role as a CEO and executive coach, I have served in many roles. These include director of a large major university center in my late 20s; upper-level leadership in a large public university; author of numerous published articles and two widely used psychological tests; and co-owner of a financial service firm, which I sold to devote myself to elevating the purpose of business by working directly with CEOs and upper-level leaders in business and industry.

It was primarily from my vantage point of my various roles in large institutional settings that I began to see how important it was to get buy-in from boards, CEOs, and presidents in the pursuit of changing the culture of an organization. I repeatedly witnessed vice-presidents, associate vice-presidents, and middle management put forth energy, creativity, and innovative strategies for improving institutional effectiveness and health—efforts that received surface encouragement from top leadership but no real support when it was time to take prudent risks and commit resources.

Truly many organizations do not take advantage of the knowledge, experience, and intellectual capital that is offered by the level of management just below the top. To make matters worse, many organizations spend hundreds of thousands of dollars on nationally recognized consultants who basically reinforce the views of top leadership. A large component of that view is driven by self-preservation, not based on what is possible for them or their organization. In fact, it is based on some early ideas about themselves that were actually in place before their brains had fully developed. By relying on these early views, they define *what they know* about themselves as *what is knowable* about them, and as a consequence sell both themselves and their organization short. In other words, the mental models of those top leaders do not allow them to see that their restricted view of their own potential limits the potential they can see and encourage in others. They don't know that "all things change when we do" (Whyte, 2002, p. 93). Frequently, consultants deliver a comprehensive package for change that ensures no meaningful change will occur. Ironically, healthy energy is often reduced within the organization; conformity and compliance are rewarded while symptoms of unhappiness and reduced commitment are generated. We value loyalty to an individual, rather than loyalty to the concepts that can make our organization great.

Unlike many of my respected colleagues at upper-leadership levels, I had the advantage of psychological training. As a result, I was able to self-comfort by virtue of understanding how it was possible for intelligent leaders to limit themselves and their organizations as a result of largely unconscious forces within them. I would ask myself, what would it be like if these leaders were open to greater possibilities in themselves and their institutions? The answer was simple: their life would be better, and their effectiveness would improve and have a positive impact on the overall success of the entire organization.

10

So what keeps this from happening in so many organizations headed by well-intentioned, intelligent, highly skilled people?

As this book will make clear, the answer is self-knowledge, a concept alluded to frequently but rarely understood as it applies to business effectiveness. Few of the most popular business books give this important concept more than a passing mention. In essence, an individual's self-knowledge reflects his or her understanding of how his or her mind, including emotions, works. Therefore, increasing individuals' self-knowledge enables them not only to see themselves—their strengths and weaknesses—more clearly but also to see other team members more realistically. Commitment, cooperation, and communication increase to levels not previously achieved. As a result, productivity naturally increases without strain.

I believe there are at least four major reasons that self-knowledge is not a major focus for business leaders: (a) the people who are experts in business are rarely the same people who are experts in understanding human psychological functioning; (b) many individuals who write about psychological functioning in work environments are researchers who often lack applied experience in helping people obtain greater personal mastery based on self-knowledge; (c) many who seek leadership positions are attracted to power for reasons other than the application of love to their work and thus are destined to recapitulate their emotional histories in the work setting; and (d) many leaders don't realize the benefit of acquiring greater self-knowledge—and, even armed with that knowledge, some still don't believe they need it.

This book is fundamentally different from many business books because it addresses the elephant in the room: that a primary asset and limitation in any organization is top leadership. Specifically, it looks at how objectively they are able to see themselves and others and to use that knowledge to enliven the health of the enterprise to accomplish its purpose efficiently.

I recall a personal conversation with the late M. Scott Peck, MD, bestselling author of *The Road Less Traveled* (1985) and other works, in which he shared his view that the best leaders are those who accept leadership positions reluctantly. In essence, they recognize the awesome responsibility of leadership and focus on how best to free those in the organization to function at their best. These reluctant leaders sense at a deep level that they must liberate their own capability before they will know how to do this for others. In other words, they must transform themselves before they can understand how to transform the organization.

In his book on organizational health, *The Advantage: Why Organizational Health Trumps Everything Else in Business* (2012), Patrick Lencioni writes, "the seminal difference between successful companies and mediocre or unsuccessful ones has little, if anything, to do with what they know or how smart they are; it has everything to do with how healthy they are" (p. 8). Like many who seek to improve organizational health and effectiveness, Lencioni identifies desirable characteristics and suggests some ways to achieve them that result in competitive advantage: "The healthier an organization is, the more of its intelligence it is able to tap into and use. Most organizations exploit only a fraction of the knowledge, experience, and intellectual capital that is available to them. But the healthy ones tap into almost all of it" (p. 11).

How is a healthy organization created?

Many business books offer models that identify external factors to address in the hope of changing people's behavior and thus improving organizational effectiveness. Some authors, like Lencioni, get very close to illuminating the power of leadership self-knowledge and even suggest a step or two that can be taken in that direction. For example, he asserts that leaders "must be the first to do the hardest things, like demonstrating vulnerability, provoking conflict, confronting people about their behavior, or calling their direct reports out when they're putting themselves ahead of the team" (p. 191). The big issue here is *how these hard things are accomplished*. A leader with limited self-knowledge would execute these tasks very differently than a leader with considerable self-knowledge. I can think of various CEOs and other business leaders who would implement the same steps toward building a cohesive team but achieve very different outcomes!

I agree that the health of an organization is vital but think that an organization's health is dependent on the health of its members, particularly those who are in positions of leadership. As Lencioni states, "There is just no escaping the fact that the single biggest factor determining whether an organization is going to get healthier—or not—is the genuine commitment and active involvement of the person in charge" (p. 190). Active involvement can take different forms—for example, actively listening can be just as valuable as actively speaking—but the key is participating in an *active* manner. The problem is that people in charge will interpret all this good advice based on what they know about themselves and others. Our purpose at CEOEffectiveness, LLC is to help business leaders maximize their effectiveness by taking key steps to improve their self-knowledge. CEOs can provide an example of the value of self-knowledge to the entire enterprise, thereby helping to move the organization toward health. When CEOs and team members at all levels achieve a realistic view of themselves, they are more likely to execute these critical steps for improving the health of their organization without doing harm. Commenting on leadership teams in organizations, Lencioni writes: "It's kind of like a family. If the parents' relationship is dysfunctional, the family will be too. That's not to say that some good things can't come out of it; it just means the family/company will not come anywhere close to realizing its full potential" (p. 19).

Self-knowledge takes time, effort, and courage—and the temporary suspension of our egos—but leads to greater results and thus more satisfaction. It is based on a deep understanding of how your mind works, including your emotions, strengths, limitations, values, and motives (Goleman, Boyatzis, & McKee, 2002). And this new knowledge must be personalized to your own circumstances. Therefore, it may take more than one reading of this book and some reflective thinking before you can develop a full appreciation of what is at stake and what must be done. Its lessons are worth the wait—the end result can be a sound appreciation of the value of self-knowledge, perhaps the best business strategy and set of skills available to any CEO or corporate leader.

Self-knowledge is acquired slowly.

By the time we know enough to understand that we contribute to our perspective and experience, a lot of neurological circuitry is already in place. This circuitry was constructed gradually, beginning with our earliest experiences, and has determined how we see ourselves and our relationship with the world. Even after we realize that some of our behavioral and emotional habits are costly and self-limiting, changing them is still very difficult. In many cases, it is only after the cost of ignoring less-than-optimal thinking and emotional habits becomes obvious that we grow curious about ourselves and our enduring patterns of behavior. If we have the courage to keep questioning everything we know about ourselves—and how we have come to believe it—we can begin to influence those neurological circuits in ways that can effect personal mastery and interpersonal effectiveness in our lives.

The greatest obstacle to achieving this may actually be the relative successes—achievements that result from a narrow focus based on mental models established earlier in life—business leaders have experienced. I am reminded of a discussion panel of Fortune 500 CEOs I attended several years ago. They all seemed to agree that when a new CEO comes aboard, he or she is usually able to improve things by squeezing more out of the 30% effort that the workforce brings to work. However, this still leaves 70% of potential largely untapped. When we fail to be curious about our own untapped potential, we define both business and personal success too narrowly; in fact, we may even believe that we and others are doing our very best.

Too often businesses focus solely on pursuing outcome measures (e.g., revenues, market share) rather than developing meaningful goals that can be believed in and shared by everyone in the company. Unfortunately, when outcome measures become destinations in themselves, the entire enterprise is maimed by the absence of a shared vision—something worth believing in—and the corporate culture suffers. As a consequence, these outcome measures can warp the very means developed to achieve them and lead to expressions of negativity, such as reduced commitment, creativity, and innovation, throughout the entire organization.

We must first know ourselves.

Perhaps no introduction to this work is more fitting than the words of Dr. W. Edwards Deming, who is quoted in the introduction to the revised edition (2006) of *The Fifth Discipline* by Peter Senge:

> Our prevailing system of management has destroyed our people. People are born with intrinsic motivation, self-respect, dignity, curiosity to learn, joy in learning. The forces of destruction begin with toddlers—a prize for the best Halloween costume, grades in school, gold stars—and on up through the university. On the job, people, teams, and divisions are ranked, reward for the top, punishment for the bottom. Management by objectives, quotas, incentive pay, business plans, put together separately, division by division, cause further loss, unknown and unknowable. (p. xii)

This quote alludes to the fact that every system and being, including humans, must be anchored in something greater than itself if it seeks to enjoy the fulfillment of a greater life. We must first know ourselves in order to make best use of our talents and abilities. The human spirit can transcend what it sees—and thinks it knows—only when it demonstrates the courage to know itself differently. It is almost impossible to do this when it is dangerous to question our long-standing mental models. It is probably not possible to accurately remember a time when we had fuller access to our broader potentials—before our compromises led us to develop these relatively enduring models of our world. Since these models were likely based on brain development that was still in progress, it is necessary to rediscover our truer selves from an adult perspective. It is very difficult to accomplish this alone, since it requires seeing ourselves in a new and different way. A common variation on an Albert Einstein quote[1] says that "No problem can be solved from the same level of consciousness that created it."

In the following sections, I will briefly describe why it is so difficult to access our fuller potential and what organizations and individuals can do to close the gap between functioning levels and innate capacity. This research-supported path can lead business executives to vital, disconfirming experiences that can widen access to their own potential. It represents a bridge between my work as a consulting psychologist and my work as an executive coach and presents practical steps that you can follow to access more of your innate capacity.

---

[1] The actual quote is "A new type of thinking is essential if mankind is to survive and move toward higher levels" (Einstein, 1946) but, as many Einstein quotes do, it has evolved over time into a slightly catchier and related yet actually inaccurate version (Varey, 2009).

Different Beginnings, Masterful Finishes: Transcending Imposed Limitations

Too often we confuse our functioning level with what we are capable of accomplishing. As a consequence, many of us have self-limiting expectations about what is possible. With greater clarity, we can be more than we ever thought we could be.

It is not the thing you fear that you must deal with, it is the *mother* of the thing you fear.

What does it take...to accept our own irrationality and the sober fact that we each bring it with us into the workplace and make far-reaching decisions based on ghostlike insecurities?

David Whyte, 2002

Early life experiences are not important simply because of their direct consequences. They also affect the construction of our enduring view of ourselves and others, a view that is created to make sense of what we experienced. In my case, a history of stability, love, and safety was quickly shattered by an overpowering event—spinal meningitis—at age seven, an event significant enough to change my internal model of the world and my place in it. Like most, I was unaware that I was now involved in a "construction project" that would influence everything that followed in my life.

The brain is constantly updating itself to incorporate new experiences. Shifting my relatively consistent view of myself as an important person who was valued and protected by his parents to one that reflected a state of helplessness, pain, and fear changed everything. My premorbid history—and the fact that I got excellent medical care, which allowed me to emerge with an intact body and mind—crucially informed the manner in which I coped. I lived through a nightmare of high fevers (peaking at 105 degrees Fahrenheit), barely tolerable pain, powerful medications, and separation from my parents, from whom I'd never been apart before my weeks of medical isolation. But stability had already been established in my life, and it was my good fortune that I had parents who were totally committed to my welfare before, during, and after my illness. How I made sense of my illness and my surrounding emotions was more important and enduring than the reality of the illness—and this is what influenced the enduring circuits in my brain.

There were many ways for me to do this as I recovered from the disease. The resolution of my experience was based on many factors, most of which were outside my conscious awareness. This resolution had to be made using my existing brain circuits—circuits that had to incorporate the profound physical and psychological changes imposed by the experience of the disease itself. The way in which I came to terms with everything may have created in me a sense of mastery and efficacy, but this could only take me so far in the pursuit of excellence in my life. It was a compromise between what I had believed and what I was faced with—hence, it wasn't realistic or objectively based. It is difficult for a child whose intellectual development is ahead of his emotional development to make sense of such a fracture of innocence. In my case, which was unique only in content (a major trauma), I created an internal narrative that was both adaptive and costly, and, like most mental models (i.e., defenses), it remained largely outside consciousness. In essence, the story I told myself permitted me to relegate multiple fears and negative emotions, created by a profound loss of innocence at such an early age, to the unconscious areas of my brain. Consciously, what I told myself was something like, "I am not weak and inferior but actually superior and fortified from further illness since I have conquered such a powerful assailant. It's unlikely that I'll ever have to worry about illness again."

Had someone asked me if I believed I was subject to illness in the future, I would probably have said yes, since I knew intellectually that all human beings are vulnerable. But in practice, my actions were guided by the "emergency software upgrade" I had "downloaded" to make sense of it all, and my interpretation of events permitted me to think in ways that fortified my newly revised mental models of myself in relation to the outside world. As with all of us, my internal story became the guiding narrative of my life and helped me achieve many successes—what I now call relative successes—most of which reinforced my perceptions and kept me from seeing and knowing the real costs. It wasn't until many years later, while enrolled in psychoanalytic training to broaden my one-sided academic research-based training, that I became aware of how the world view I created when I was seven years old had influenced everything that followed. It had allowed me to "succeed" at a very early age but at a higher emotional cost than I should have paid.

———————

No human being has the option of being completely rational, even if he or she believes otherwise. The organization of the brain insures this. Whether we experience it consciously or not, emotions, which by definition are irrational, influence thought. In fact, their influence is likely greater and definitely less predictable when they influence thought outside our awareness.

Our development as human beings takes place in a context that is never completely aligned with our natural proclivities and strengths. Hence, we are forced to unknowingly make life-altering choices very early in life. Those choices push us to redefine and align our self-perception with the values and expectations of the only world we know. This foundation sets the pathway we'll follow until, at some later point in life, something inside us causes us to take a purposeful step, take creative action, toward our destiny. For those who refuse to be open to the creative fire inside them, this may never happen. These are the children who were required to give up too much of their true selves too early. As a consequence, they refused to grow older; they never relinquished their reliance on energy supplied from the outside to compensate for the barely audible screams from within. In many respects, they are grown-ups, but in other respects, they rely too much on beliefs about themselves and others established in childhood. As a consequence, they define their potential too narrowly and limit both themselves and others from moving toward their greater potentials.

Our brain has the capacity to change itself throughout our lives.
Fortunately, we are learning more and more about the highly plastic nature of the human brain. Our brain has the capacity to change itself throughout our lives. Even though the pathways laid earliest have a kind of primacy, every decision we make presents an opportunity to modify our prior learning.

Every future CEO, employee, and customer is born with many abilities, or potentials, in a number of areas. Everyone has the potential to excel in some way. In this section we'll talk about potential and why some people are so successful at recognizing and realizing their potentials and why others aren't. We are all born with similar "hardware." Our "software" is written by our individual, unique experiences, ultimately determining the potentials that we'll realize. As stated earlier, the greatest danger to self-realization may actually be relative success, especially if the payoff satisfies our conscious mind enough to reduce our curiosity about knowing ourselves further. The luckiest among us may be those who experience nagging disquiet early and take action to determine the cause. Less fortunate are those who are able to explain away what they don't want to see and allow vital time to pass. If we pay attention, we are reminded of our psychological blind spots by feedback from others and symptomatic experiences in ourselves. But knowing how they present themselves often requires deliberate actions involving honest dialogue with trusted others.

Let's look at the relationship between how we function and what we're capable of accomplishing. Picture the total of our potentials as a circle. Some people's circles are larger than others. But size is not the real issue—the much more important issue is the difference between what we think we are and what we truly are. Although all our potentials have limits, the big challenges in life and work rarely constitute these limits. Rather, we limit ourselves because we don't understand our potential, know how to gain greater access to it, or know how to translate this information into positive actions that move us toward realization.

Early stimulation: Too much or too little can cause problems.
So what stops us from gaining this access and understanding? What can we do to enlarge the gateway and release our greater potential? One only needs to observe an active toddler filled with energy, curiosity, the absence of malice, and heightened learning ability to recognize that the advantages of a beginner's mind are gradually lost over time. But why?

To understand this, we must look at our own histories. At times, our parents or caregivers rejected parts of us through criticism, inattention, or both. Over time, we learned that, in order to gain their approval, we needed to separate those aspects of ourselves from our experience and "hide" them from our own consciousness. The amount of criticism or lack of quality attention from our parents determined how much of our true selves we removed. We energized the parts of ourselves that we learned to value while restricting or limiting energy to parts of ourselves that, because of our childhood consciousness, we thought were not acceptable. The unacceptable parts are cast into the subconscious "basement" of our minds and labeled conflictual, unacceptable, or bad. I am reminded of a quote from Frederich Nietzsche: "Be careful, lest in casting out your demons you exorcise the best thing in you."

Slowly and imperceptibly, we restrict access to our broader potential. Remember that circle we talked about? Create a small circle within it. This represents the parts of ourselves that are a compromise between what we thought was acceptable to our parents and our truer selves, the parts of us that we learned to value and accept as we began to make our world smaller and smaller, starting very early in life. In other words, we learned to become what our parents or caregivers valued, even if it meant restricting access to our true potential and our true selves. The paradox here is that this process sometimes leads us to overdevelop our non-talents and underdevelop our genuine talents or gifts. This model will exert great influence in our lives, though it may remain tacit and outside of consciousness.

Another analogy may help to further clarify the point. Computers come with an operating system that represents that upper limit on the functionality of any

Functioning Level
Based on Mental Models

Untapped Potential
Based on Lack of CEO Self-Knowledge

downloaded software.[2] Analogously, we are born with multiple potentials that can be developed or discouraged by our experiences. Repeated messages can create neural circuits (i.e., "software") that determine later access to our capability. Our parents or caretakers play a large part in designing the software we will use and in determining its effect on our "operating system." Once installed, the software replaces the operating system in defining who we believe ourselves to be. These experiences and the circuits developed are part of the neurological substrate of our *mental models*, the deeply held core that influences what we believe about ourselves and others. Mental models limit access to our potential

---

[2] The CPU and memory also play a big part in defining the upper limit on a computer's potential capability. We focused on the operating system here for purposes of keeping the example more understandable for the average business reader.

and cause us to confuse functional ability with innate capacity. It is this very confusion that keeps us from gaining greater access to our larger potential and unknowingly settling for relative success. The leverage created by objective self-knowledge is enormous in both positive and negative directions, and the path to self-discovery will always require courage and openness.

Now, you can begin to have an inkling of how important leaders are to organizations and how their own limitations are mirrored throughout the entire company.

A couple of important circle-related observations can be made here.

- The influence of the large circle never completely goes away nor does the sense that we are capable of more. But over time we come to define ourselves by our smaller circle and to believe consciously that it represents the upper limit of what we are capable of accomplishing.

- The area of the large circle represents our unrealized potential. If we are fortunate, we will be reminded of its existence many times in our lives as it glints and winks at us in the pauses of our life.

- Many leaders are aware of their limitations and assume they are unchangeable. Yet in the back of their mind, they also sense their greater potential.

So, our large circle (our potential) presses for expression and exerts a kind of gravity on the smaller circle. If ignored, it can create symptoms like boredom, anxiety, anger, or depression, which lurk on the outside, knocking on the door of our awareness. The way we interpret and respond to that knock often becomes the theme of our life. And even though we actively hide the removed parts of ourselves from our consciousness, their influence never completely goes away.

With the passage of time, we learn to deny our real needs and create defenses to keep them out of our conscious awareness. While defenses may be necessary and create a guiding narrative for our lives, they can be helpful or maladaptive. Over time, we have broader experiences that offer us opportunities to develop more complicated and adaptive defenses. But some of these defenses may cost us dearly. They often rob us of our energy and keep us from seeing the big picture of our lives.

What can be achieved without the burden of extra weight?
So how does this affect business leaders who must deal with other people and organizations? What is it like to achieve relative success and be unaware of our unrealized potential? To answer these questions we must begin to look at ourselves and others in a different way.

Knowing what happens inside other people and especially inside us is critical if we hope to experience more than limited effectiveness (i.e., relative success) in our organization. An illustration may help elucidate. Imagine a swimmer in a timed two-person heat who reaches the finish line before his competitor. Unlike in routine heats, each swimmer in this competition carries an invisible 5-lb. weight on each wrist and ankle. If neither swimmer has ever swum without the extra weights, or is unaware that they are there (i.e., tacit mental models), the competition and victory would likely seem to be a *normal* measure of their performance level for that event. By virtue of the victory, the winner of this "invisible 20-lb." race would be in a position to compete with winners from other, similar competitions. Based on training, skill, and knowledge, record times would be cut shorter and shorter for these events over time. Fans would be impressed at the competitors' athletic prowess and record race times. Finally, the best of the best would be identified (i.e., those who moved from good to great) as those who search for ways to further enhance their performance continue to decrease their times. But: If these top competitors never experience swimming freely, they will never know what could be achieved without the burden of extra weights. More importantly, they will never become aware that they are not swimming freely!

This example illustrates in a simplified form what happens in our personal and business lives on a daily basis. Although we may refine our ability to operate effectively in *our* world, our greater potential remains hidden from us. In some respects this is the human condition, but most of us live far more limited lives than we have to. Our mental models of ourselves and others limit us in at least two ways: First, we define ourselves too narrowly and do not even entertain the idea that our level of self-knowledge is not objective or realistic but is shaped by our unique experiences; and, second, we actively maintain illusions about ourselves and others that lead us to restrict—if not distort—the information we receive from inside and outside and to respond to both with self-talk and behaviors that are consistent with what we believe about ourselves and others.

In essence, our beliefs contribute to what we see, and we interpret what we observe as validation of what we believe.

In many respects, the uniqueness of our family unit and the trauma inherent in socialization determine how open we are to objective self-knowledge. In turn, this influences our awareness of "others" as separate objects. Our culture influences the direction of our human struggle to reclaim our complete selves, but the options that are most appealing to us, and the risks we are willing to take, are ultimately a reflection of our relationship with ourselves. Even the way we respond to a truth is telling. In the words of David J. Lieberman, "A truth that you acknowledge does not offend, nor does a lie that you know to be false. Only a truth that you don't want to recognize as such causes you pain" (1997, p. 280).

In essence, we are all like the weighted-down swimmers to some degree, required to expend unnecessary (and often depleting) energy to remain at the top of our game. As long as our competition is similarly encumbered, we can still successfully compete in our particular invisible 20-lb. race.

But what if our competition discovers the weights and realizes their pointlessness? He or she would accomplish the same feat faster, more easily, and more comfortably. We would become painfully aware of the benefit that self-knowledge confers and the value it adds to successful outcomes.

Our mental models function as gatekeepers.
What our mental models do not allow us to see is as important, if not more so, than what our mental models allow us to experience. They're like invisible gatekeepers who not only choose what may enter but also interpret the significance of what is admitted. These filters ultimately lead to our behavior, which is then experienced by others based on their models of the world and their place in it. No wonder many of us are exhausted at the end of the day.

So much of our energy is unavailable for more satisfying creative endeavors because it is used to maintain our subjective self-image and preserve what we believe is possible within that framework. From the perspective of our experience, we are responding to reality realistically and can offer ample evidence of the many good decisions we have made within our constructed context, designed to support our rarely challenged beliefs. This is relative success. Problematic is that many of us believe that what we have not discovered in ourselves does not exist, and nothing could be further from the truth. Our psychological defenses collaborate with our mental models to keep us from knowing a greater clarity about ourselves.

We define who we are by our direct experience, which is often based on the application of a very limited fraction of our true potential. Our mental models identify what is possible within their scope but simultaneously prevent us from seeing what is possible beyond the psychological blinders we developed much earlier in our lives. Our achievement is measured against what we believe about ourselves and our abilities. In other words, our mental models influence what we see and our interpretation of what we see and, based on these, determine our performance. When our models are good enough to produce gratifying results, we persist and move in that direction. For the fortunate among us, this is not enough. They often experience a longing for something more and a sense that something is missing from their lives.

A comparison between self-knowledge and a healthy immune system can offer some clarity. The immune system is the brain of the body. In fact, we now know that the immune system can learn. The link between the immune system and the central nervous system is the focus of the relatively new field of psychoneuroimmunology. The nervous system's connection to the immune system is essential to the latter's proper function. The chemical messengers that operate most extensively in both the brain and the immune system are most dense in areas that regulate emotion. There is no psychological state that is not in some way mimicked by the immune system.

In many cases, it is the health-preserving immune system rather than the pathogens themselves that generate the most disruptive symptoms. It is the body's striving for health that makes us feel so terrible when we experience the flu or a cold virus. Like a chronic illness, our limited access to our unrealized potential prevents full functional access to our multiple capabilities. These "disowned" parts of us, which have the potential to enlarge our access to ourselves, often generate feelings (e.g., disinterest, exhaustion, distraction) analogous to the physical symptoms our immune system produces.

Do these feelings and unwanted states represent a longing for the unrecognized and unacknowledged parts of ourselves that we no longer know?

One can see in others only what is in him- or herself. The more fixed a person's behavior tends to be, the less differentiated are the responses they receive from others. Healthy, mature individuals live in a differentiated world where they are constantly offered opportunities to expand their perspective and to challenge their fixed social constructions regarding themselves and others. When others feel free to be creative and express themselves fully in our presence, this is a measure of *our* psychological health and maturity—plus, it's very good for business. I would go one step further here and say that in the knowledge-based world of the future, it is essential for business.

Most of us experience only a fraction of our potential and retain our parental (and other) injunctions in the timeless part of our mind. Even though it's silent, this part of our mind continues to signal to our awareness that we are living only a part of our true potential. When this concept is carried over to your business, it becomes clear that it also may be achieving only a fraction of its full potential.

This concept is beautifully summarized by Marianne Williamson: "Our deepest fear is not that we are inadequate. Our deepest fear is that we are powerful beyond measure. It is our light, not our darkness, that most frightens us… Your playing small does not serve the world" (1992, p. 190). This illustrates a glimpse of awareness without consciousness. Somehow we sense that we have more potential than we can functionally access but are afraid to believe it. Ironically, fear of our own greatness is what keeps many of us from realizing our full potential.

In practice, this may lead some high-level executives to engage in self-sabotaging behavior when they experience tangible success. It's almost as though we have an internal governor that constantly keeps our success regulator at a comfortable level. For example, a top-level executive whose strengths were never acknowledged by a narcissistic father was driven to extremely high levels of achievement to disprove his father's low appraisal of him. Since his high level of achievement was driven by unresolved anger toward his father, it negatively affected his general mood, led to unrealistic expectations of direct reports, and contributed to an oversensitivity to his customers' purchasing decisions. As a consequence, his considerable achievements brought him little joy, and others experienced fear, anxiety, and powerlessness in his presence. In short, he created the same emotional environment in his organization that he had experienced as a child—and he had virtually no awareness of this.

The company experienced relative success in the short run but gradually lost market share and was subsequently acquired by another company for a fraction of its potential value.

Another CEO, who inherited his company in his late 20s when his father unexpectedly died, was nearing retirement. He put the company up for sale with a business broker who had been able to negotiate an atypically good price with exceptional terms from a willing buyer who had been vetted. Although the deal was remarkably good objectively, the CEO could not bring himself to accept the deal. It was only after he was queried on his reaction to his father's death that he realized he had never grieved the loss of his beloved parent and that the company itself was a way of keeping his father close. Fortunately, he made the connection in time—the business brokerage market collapsed six months after the transaction was completed.

Our brain sometimes makes things even harder.

Achieving self-awareness is made even more difficult by two hardwired brain tendencies identified by neuroscientist Robert K. Cooper (2001b, 2006). First, we tend to interpret ambiguity as danger. Second, when faced with stress, we tend to increase the intensity, frequency, and duration of habitual responses. Put simply, we play it safe, and if we're tempted to seek greater clarity, we rev up the defenses to insure that emotional insight does not occur.

How can we ever escape our small-circle, manufactured self, surrounded by defenses to keep us from knowing and experiencing our true potential? Later, we'll take a look at why this level of understanding is especially critical to business effectiveness and success in the knowledge-based global world. But before we get into that, let's briefly explore the qualities and values of leadership that have stood the test of time.

What Have We Learned?

- Every future CEO, employee, and customer is born with multiple capacities in a number of areas. The total of these potentials can be represented by a circle.

- The big challenge in life is gaining greater access to the potential we already have.

- The advantages of a beginner's mind are gradually lost with the passage of time.

- The path to self-discovery always requires courage and openness.

- A small circle within the large circle represents the parts of ourselves that are a compromise between what we thought was acceptable to our parents and our truer selves.

- We can sometimes overdevelop our non-talents and underdevelop our genuine gifts.

- The large circle presses for expression and exerts a kind of gravity on the smaller circle, creating symptoms like boredom, anxiety, anger, and depression.

- Most of us experience only a fraction of our potential.

- Ironically, fear of our own greatness is what holds many of us from realizing our full potential.

Energizing Enduring Ideas: Ourselves as Instruments of Change

A few ideas and values have been associated with leadership success in different cultures over vast periods of time. They serve as external guides until they are embedded in our brain circuitry and we are able to lead from our heart. At that point we can trust our thoughts and actions to move us and our organizations toward their potential.

I obtained my first leadership position a year after earning my PhD in clinical psychology, when I was asked to head a large staff of psychologists, psychiatrists, and other doctoral-level professionals at a major public university. I was 27 years old, and the next-youngest member of the staff was about 15 years my senior. Being asked to take on this awesome responsibility at such a young age was unexpected by my conscious mind but had been carefully planned by my unconscious mind, which had willed itself to never be vulnerable and helpless again. I had not only found an illusory way to stay physically healthy but also discovered an insurance policy against failure in other areas. Internally, I was more than confident in my resourcefulness and determined to excel beyond the expectations of others. In essence, I covered all my bases, making sure that my academic record and job performance were so stellar that the likelihood of ever getting an unwelcome surprise was as remote as possible.

Somehow, my history of parental love and vigilance born of trauma permitted me to negotiate mutually beneficial relationships with the university's upper leadership and with my colleagues. The organization thrived, even becoming a model in many ways for others across the nation, but this was achieved in a way that required too much from me at one level and not enough at another. The model of the world I created when I was seven years old was in charge, and my conscious mind had no awareness of it. The quality of my success was influenced by my level of self-knowledge at the time. It wasn't until many years later that I realized that the caliber of my relationship with myself (i.e., my levels of self-knowledge and acceptance) was also the upper limit of the caliber of the relationships that I could have with others. From an organizational point of view, this quality also significantly influenced the efforts of each person in the organization.

Those above me were delighted that my organization could deliver whatever was needed, usually ahead of time. Those who reported to me knew they could count on me to represent them and the organization in a manner that made us secure, fertile, and resource-rich. But, though my accomplishments were respected, I wasn't accomplishing them with the fullest participation of others in the organization. As a consequence, my employees were not sufficiently stimulated to stretch themselves, and, with some exceptions, they believed they could rely on me to make the tough decisions while they remained safely ensconced in their positions. This is what I call relative success. From the outside, the story is impressive. But the structure and function of our center replicated my internal narrative and the tacit mental model on which it was based. I knew what needed to be achieved and what actions would move us toward accomplishment, but I was not fully aware that there were many avenues for execution and that the one I had chosen came with a cost. I have come to believe that a leader's level of self-knowledge and how he or she relates to him- or herself represent the upper limit on what the organization can accomplish. Although we excelled as an organization, the same or a greater level of achievement could have been accomplished more joyously by modeling and empowering everyone in the organization to lead from the heart.

We've been discussing how critically important it is for you, as the head of your business, to gain greater access and understanding of your own unrealized potential. And we've also realized how our knowledge (or lack thereof) transposes to those around us. When the CEO or head of the business or organization isn't curious about him- or herself—in particular, when he or she doesn't realize that what he or she is observing in others is directly influenced by his or her leadership—any attempt at transformation is rendered impossible, at least without the help of a truly excellent psychologist. The corporate culture will likely become stagnant.

This concept can be phrased as simple equations:

CEO + no curiosity or understanding about self =
Limited capacity to observe or engage others or read clues

CEO + curiosity and understanding about self =
Enhanced capacity to observe and engage others and read clues

Remember, with the CEOs' right to lead their organizations comes responsibility to the customers, the organization, and the employees. How the CEO's intellectual and emotional intelligence affects these three entities becomes a critical factor in the culture and outcomes of the organization.

Being aware of how his or her beliefs, emotions, and actions affect others (i.e., his or her *stimulus value*) is one of the most important attributes a leader can have. Our global world is only going to become more interdependent as time passes, making the possibilities for excelling even greater. We have an abundance of knowledge gleaned from science and technology literally at our fingertips. But—and this is a big caveat—the applications of this knowledge continue to be limited by human nature, which appears to have remained essentially unchanged since the beginning of civilization.[3]

The markers that can define our course to self-knowledge are the qualities consistently associated with great leaders throughout history.

The journey within is like making a new path through the woods. At first there is little but broad markers to go on, like the height of trees, the direction of sunlight, and the placement of stars. But once we get our bearings, we can concentrate on the path itself. Our energies can become more focused on what is before us. If we intend to use the path again, it must be constructed to endure. We must know it from several perspectives so that, despite situational changes that occur over time, we can recognize it and opt to take it. Becoming a better leader means becoming more effective and may require us to rely initially on some aspirational markers that can only broadly define our course. Ideally, like the sun and tall trees, these will stand the test of time and apply to all who choose to forge the path to their greater selves.

Our search for these enduring markers leads us back to the beginning, to take a good, hard look at the trans-cultural qualities of great leaders throughout history. Our goal is only to extract the wisdom that can serve as a guide throughout the process of recapturing our nascent potentials. Our world is globally interconnected, and it is increasingly important to learn from the successes and failures of other leaders anchored to civilizations of the past. Harvard-educated historian J. Rufus Fears created a remarkable series of 36 lectures entitled *The Wisdom of History* (2007). These lectures identify qualities that have consistently been associated with great leaders representing many different cultures since the beginning of civilization: (a) a bedrock of principles, (b) a moral compass, (c) a vision, and (d) the ability to build a consensus to achieve that vision.

---

[3] Because human nature has been viewed by many as unchangeable, most people assume its effects are givens and work around them. This is a huge mistake for knowledge-based companies because the human brain is designed to override the archaic tendencies that manifest themselves with great regularity in unexamined lives. A few cutting-edge thinkers recognize this, and their thoughts are represented throughout this work.

Dr. Fears observed that history is a quest for universal values and notes that common values have been recognized by nations around the world. In his words, "we find that such values as wisdom, justice, courage, and moderation are the basis of a moral and successful life" (p. 186). Along with truth, these values are essential components of developing a formula for leadership strength and are closely aligned with self-knowledge, leadership effectiveness, and recapturing lost potential. These qualities and values were present in civilizations that thrived for the longest periods of time. And, even more interesting, they align very closely with contemporary research on the neuroscience of leadership (as revealed by Robert K. Cooper) and the disciplines that must be mastered in order to create learning organizations (as discussed by Peter Senge). We will take a look at both areas later.

Interestingly, Fears says that the Greeks identified our greatest sin or shortcoming as "hubris," or the abuse of the weak by the strong. He interprets hubris as a type of immorality associated with the abuse of power. Contemporarily, we might associate hubris with excess, grandiosity, arrogance, false pride, and narcissism—but none of these fully capture the true meaning. Hubris can be contrasted with humility and is the cause of much wasted energy associated with the misuse of institutional power.

Unrealized potential can be converted into energy.

Neuroscience and psychology are making great strides at illuminating why human nature seems to have remained unchanged throughout history and how unrealized potential can be liberated and converted into kinetic energy.[4] And where does all this lead us? It takes us straight to a future when designing organizations that are capable of learning, changing, and innovating is a reality.

That future is within our grasp.

---

[4] Potential energy is stored energy—think of a parked car filled with fuel. Kinetic energy is the energy of motion. For example, a ball held at an elevation relative to a lower elevation has potential energy that can be converted into kinetic energy on its release.

—————What Have We Learned?—————

- Becoming aware of our own stimulus value is indispensable.

- Science and technology have created abundant knowledge, but its application continues to be limited by human nature.

- The qualities of great leaders identified by Dr. Fears are (a) a bedrock of principles, (b) a moral compass, (c) a vision, and (d) the ability to build a consensus to achieve that vision.

- The characteristics of great leaders are truth, wisdom, justice, courage, and moderation.

- The Greeks identified hubris, or the abuse of the weak by the strong, as our greatest sin or shortcoming.

- Knowledge from neuroscience and psychology are beginning to illuminate why human nature seems to have remained unchanged throughout history and how unrealized potential can be liberated and converted into kinetic energy.

- Designing organizations that are capable of learning, changing, and innovating is within our reach.

Rediscovering Ourselves: The Path to Self-Knowledge

The path to accessing our potential and putting more of our capability to use involves an internal struggle. Part of us wants to know more, but another wants to believe we already know enough. Unless we are dedicated to reality at all cost, what is familiar may hold sway.

There were two aspects of my leadership that may have seemed contradictory to others. I was committed to and protective of those who worked for me. But at the same time, my awareness of the conditions that could expand my employees' capacity to do great work was more closely linked to my mental models and defenses than their needs. My early traumatic history and the sudden loss of innocence accompanying it limited the ways in which my conscious good intentions could be delivered.

My self-model in relation to others reflected the major themes from my early life: first, authority figures were devoted, sincere, and honest; and second, I was resilient and needed to be overscrupulous to insure that nothing negative happened to me or those entrusted to me within the organization. Only the first assumption was conscious. My mental model of invulnerability energized my positive drive, confidence, and striving for excellence. But my need to maintain immunity from illness, vulnerability, and disappointment constricted my view and my emotions. How could I offer others what my venerated parents had given me when my delivery system was encumbered?

High drive, good intentions, and a commitment to be fair and just to others is not enough if you are looking though lenses you've created to protect yourself from disruptive or painful feelings. If your defenses keep you from knowing yourself as you truly are, they are also limiting your access to your full potential—even if your achievements and successes are genuinely impressive. Others may be similarly limited, but their circumstances and limitations differ; consequently, they can enlighten us if we are willing to listen to and observe them with a *beginner's mind*. I needed to develop myself before I could understand what I could do to contribute to others' development and liberate more of their potential.

At work, I was more willing to take care of others and deliver the goods than to see others as having the capacity to teach me about myself. As a consequence, I was the "captain of the ship"—and the primary energy source of the organization. But I was unable to see how this tendency discouraged others from becoming curious about themselves and offering their best. The outside world often conspires to keep leaders from knowing themselves as they truly are, and under this condition the organization can never reach its full potential or be fully alive.

The critical importance of self-knowledge to personal mastery and thus optimal business effectiveness is not easy to see and even more difficult to understand. Many consider self-knowledge to be an abstract concept that sounds good but doesn't directly relate to business effectiveness in any practical way. Others believe they already know themselves fairly well and that their time and energy should instead be focused on business oversight and execution. They can point to years, maybe decades, of business success that seemingly demonstrate their knowledge of themselves, others, and how the world operates, therefore validating this perception.

Early impressions leave lasting traces.
But when it comes to self-knowledge, a little bolstered by relative success is sometimes a dangerous thing. Confident in our self-knowledge, we tend to ascribe our beliefs, thoughts, and emotions with power and assume that they are based on an accurate and precise view of reality. As the image that opened this section illustrates, if we enjoy a position of power, the interpersonal part of our world often cooperates in helping us maintain this illusion. The following visual analogy will help clarify how this seemingly abstract concept operates in the real world.

Imagine that, not long after birth, very powerful lenses (as powerful as binocular lenses) were permanently stitched in front of each eye so that distances appeared shorter and objects closer than they actually are. Assume that the lenses remain firmly implanted for several years. These powerful lenses allow your visual/spatial experiences and their impressions on your developing brain to be very different from your experience without the lenses. Early impressions leave lasting traces. As these impressions are fortified by later experiences, they become part of our basis for subjective reality.

What might happen as this infant becomes a toddler and later an adult? Picture someone who is standing 10 or 20 feet away from you but who appears to be standing right in front of you. If you wanted to shake his hand, you would need to walk some distance to do so. Over time you would become accustomed to the discrepancy and would know just when to reach out to shake his hand— probably after you had walked the anticipated distance, expecting to be able to grasp his hand but finding that he still looked somewhat blurry!

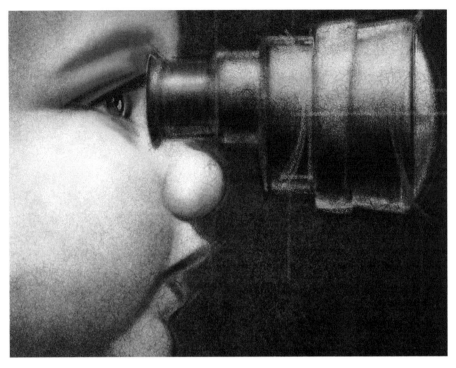

As you grow and develop looking through these lenses, you begin to encode experiences at various locations in your brain. Neurological circuits and pathways are created, and a knowledge base of connections is constructed. Gradually, you are able to know and anticipate your transactions as you become more and more skilled at mapping the internal and external world based on what you see and experience.

If we stretch this analogy to include all our senses, perceptions, and beliefs, we begin to approximate something closer to our actual development experience. Over time and with many successful experiences, we begin to develop a sense of mastery based on our *unique* connections with the world. These experiences eventually become the basis for the mental models that will serve as templates of what we have learned and how we behave in the future. Although we are sometimes conscious of these models, they also operate outside our awareness. For some very smart people, becoming aware of the lenses can be postponed for a long time, perhaps into middle or even old age. The parts that remain outside our awareness continue to have an influence on our thoughts, beliefs, and actions.

This concept is not so different from the unconscious brain circuits that permit us to walk and run without conscious intention. But when it comes to thoughts, emotions, and actions, we act more like Monday-morning quarterbacks. Our mind becomes adept at accounting for our actions even when our explanations represent a significant deviation from the truth.

We can't rely on the same perceptions that created our mental models.

At first, the process of learning to walk is slow. It takes a lot of energy and concentration. However, once the circuits are firmly in place, walking becomes mostly automatic, permitting us to make more efficient use of our time and energy. Likewise, relying on our mental models in the social-evaluative parts of life helps us accomplish things more efficiently. But, unlike with motor skills, practice in these areas of our life doesn't necessarily lead to optimal functioning or performance. Instead, optimal performance depends on how closely our mental models approximate reality. We can't know this by relying on the same perceptions that created the mental models in the first place.

So, how does this relate to self-knowledge? Over our life span, we draw conclusions about ourselves and how we might improve our lives. As we develop a concept of ourselves in relation to our world, we begin to challenge ourselves in unique ways. As a result, we are able to develop specialized abilities, skills, and knowledge that eventually become incorporated into our definition of ourselves. In fact, we may begin to think that we know ourselves pretty well as we refine our skills and begin to reliably anticipate the consequences of our actions. But that knowledge has been acquired through the metaphorical lenses that have silently and imperceptibly influenced our transactions with the world since birth. We've been looking through them for so long that we believe we're actually looking through clear glass. Although the lenses were necessary to get us launched in life, they are not the fuel that will take us into the orbit of our true destiny. To discover that purpose, we must go back to the original equipment; in the words of T.S. Elliot (1943): "We shall not cease from exploration. And the end of all our exploring will be to arrive where we started and know the place for the first time" (p. 47).

I'll let you in on a now-obvious dirty little secret. Everyone leaves his birth setting with those metaphorical lenses firmly sutured to his eyes. In other words, no one leaves the birth setting on his own. He leaves it in the care of some person or persons, usually a parent or family member in whose care his life will be entrusted. Human beings develop slowly and become independent over a long period of time. During this process, they must literally reside somewhere. One person's "somewhere" can be very different from another's. Believe me: I have spent over two decades working with extremely successful and high functioning people; none of their histories are what society considers "optimal." I have come to believe that optimal functioning can be acquired only through courage and determination. This is where the lenses come in.

If this seems like a stretch, let's connect the dots. All humans use these lenses in a variety of ways in order to limit and even relinquish parts of ourselves to maintain a relationship with a parent or caretaker. We have to accommodate the beliefs, values, habits, and proclivities of those who make the rules governing our early life. Despite the fact that life is cumulative, our early experiences tend to have a disproportionate influence on virtually everything that occurs afterward. In short, our mental models are constructed from our perception of reality as we know it. They are born from our earliest learning experiences. Problematic is that self-knowledge will elude us to the extent that we are able to access only limited parts of our capabilities—and they may not be the best parts! Likely, our mental models represent a compromise between the unencumbered bundle of joy our parents took home from the hospital and the parts of us that aligned with parental expectations.

A lofty life task is to recapture the missing parts of ourselves for the benefit of ourselves and others. This process involves psychological and spiritual growth and the intention of rising above what was handed to us by perhaps well-intentioned caretakers, who may have subconsciously thought that we were less than we actually were. But no amount of insight gained through hard work or self-reflection can accomplish this if our mental models restrict our capacity for realistic self-knowledge. It is only after we become aware of the lenses and understand that removing them requires not only wisdom, courage, moderation, and compassion but also the cooperation of trusted others that we join a trajectory to gaining real self-knowledge.

Subconsciously, we know there is more in life than what we have settled for.
There is little in life that is more exhilarating than seeing something for the first time that has been there all along. Like welcoming back an old friend

thought forever lost, this is an adventure that can lead us to redefine personal mastery in the process of rediscovering ourselves.

Frequently, we sense that we have the potential for a greater life, but our tendency to continue on the tried-and-true path keeps us from knowing it consciously. We desperately want to keep the familiar lenses on because everything we have learned about ourselves and others has been encoded through them. Something in each of us struggles to awaken our consciousness to the realization that there is more than what we have settled for. This "something" is an invitation from our greater self. The voice may be barely discernible at first but will gradually begin to be heard. It is simply telling us to participate more completely in our own lives until the parts of us that have been asleep are awakened and available to fully engage.

Ultimately, the way we choose to resolve that struggle becomes our life. Happiness is the feeling state signaling that we are on the right path. But the path to happiness is fraught with warning signs like anxiety, fear, anger, and depression. We all drive through yellow lights. But when a symbolic yellow light signals that we are about to embark on an adventure of self-realization, our design encourages us to slow down. At this point, too many of us stop the journey altogether to avoid facing the enormous vulnerability that comes with questioning what we think we know about ourselves in favor of reality.

Research suggests that exploration of the different options presented by life is an important component of human happiness. In many ways, our lives are the result of a power struggle in our brain. Self-knowledge is the product of engaging in that struggle against our natural tendency to return to a more comfortable course.

What Have We Learned?

- A little self-knowledge bolstered by relative success goes a long way.

- As we grow and develop, experiences are encoded at various locations in our brains.

- We develop a sense of mastery based on our unique connections with the world.

- Our minds become adept at accounting for our own actions, even when our explanations are less than truthful.

- Optimal performance depends on how closely our mental models approximate reality.

- Our early experiences have a disproportionate influence on everything that occurs afterward.

- Mental models represent a compromise between the unencumbered newborn and the parts of us that aligned with parental expectation. We are faced with the task of recapturing the missing parts of ourselves.

- We sense our greater potential, but tend to continue on the tried-and-true path and thus are kept from consciously knowing it.

Business Response...ability:
Timely Reality-Based Execution

Competition often points us outside of our sphere of influence and causes us to lose focus on what is right before us and in our control. Pursuing excellence in ourselves and our organization contributes to competitive advantage, and competitive advantage is often an outcome of pursuing excellence.

My definition of responsibility led me to stay current in my field, honor my commitments, and do my very best to insure that our organization was nationally recognized, at the cutting edge of service delivery, and valuable to its broader enterprise. As an organization, we were responsible for making sure that all constituencies were satisfied, if not impressed.

A number of indices established that we were one of the best centers in our field in the country. I had coauthored the most psychometrically sophisticated test of college adjustment in the country and had coauthored another, similar test for use in employee assistance programs (EAPs). Our professional staff was highly trained and enjoyed the highest levels of national accreditation available for service and training.

That's why being curious about my unrealized potential seemed like an unnecessary diversion. There was work to be done, and all the feedback said that we were on the right track; in fact, we were succeeding beyond anyone's expectations. When we compared our performance to that of other, similarly positioned centers, there seemed to be no reason to stray from our successful formula. In short, we were focused on a proven process, one that we knew led to rewards and recognition, rather than our unrealized potential, and our shared paradigm limited our access to the greater creativity, energy, innovation, and commitment that remained untapped in our organization.

Many top business leaders define their responsibility to include communicating with internal and external constituencies, making high-level decisions about policy and strategy, advising the board of directors, and driving change within the organization to achieve competitive advantage. These and other top-level responsibilities are likely to be executed very differently by different leaders. More important, the same leader may execute these responsibilities very differently at different points in his or her career, depending on the level of self-knowledge he or she is enjoying. Relative success can be achieved with limited self-knowledge, but an organization that can create its own future requires something different from its leaders.

Personal mastery must be an assigned responsibility for the leader who truly wants to be effective.

How many organizations include in the list of leadership's responsibilities "improving top leadership's personal effectiveness at energizing management, workers, and customers toward achieving the corporate vision?" Self-knowledge is a prerequisite to personal mastery and requires that we align our mental models of ourselves and others with objective reality. Even the leader's commitment to move in this direction is detectable by others in the organization. As a consequence, they become much more willing to freely commit their energies to achieving the organizational purpose. Leaders who assign themselves the responsibility of personal mastery will have "the wind at their back" in a manner they did not anticipate. In turn, their ability to respond appropriately to others and stimulate positive energy from constituents is refined.

Before we continue our look at great leaders, let's revisit our circle analogy. Most of us live our lives guided by our small circle, considering our greater untapped potential (i.e., our large circle) unknowable or unimaginable. Unless we encounter an obstacle that requires more from us than we are used to, many of us are not curious about our unrealized potential; instead, we're satisfied defining ourselves as the smaller circle, with which we're familiar and comfortable. Consequently, we spend our available energy improving the effectiveness of who we believe ourselves to be. Naturally, we choose to surround ourselves with people who are operating similarly. What about the rest of our energy? Sadly, most of it is consumed keeping our large circle outside our conscious awareness.

We can achieve high levels of performance by relying on our small circles, but the cost to our lives and those affected by our actions can be very high. Illness and death are potential consequences for the leader who experiences *extremely* high levels of drive. Extremely high levels of achievement almost always come at the expense of other areas of our personality. This "small circle achievement," which can look quite impressive from the outside, is very different from the achievement that results from accessing your greater innate potential.

What part does motivation play?

In his book *The Genius in All of Us* (2011), David Shenk notes that "…deep motivation can have more than one possible origin. A person can become joyfully inspired, spiritually devoted, or deeply resentful; motivation can be selfish or vengeful, or arise out of desperation to prove someone right or wrong; it can be conscious or unconscious" (p. 119). But when it comes to performance, the source of our motivation may be as important as the level of our motivation, especially when it comes to its impact on the performance of others in our sphere of influence or control.

Edmund Morris' book, *Beethoven: The Universal Composer* (2005), describes the childhood experiences of Beethoven who, as a four-year-old, could barely reach the keys of the piano. If Beethoven did not play as he was told, his father beat him. His neighbors observed him "'standing in front of the clavier and weeping'" (p. 16). His options were few, and working at mastering the piano may have been his only real choice. He was under an enormous amount of continual pressure to master musical instruments and musical theory. "There were few days when he was not flogged, or locked up in the cellar. [His father] also deprived him of sleep, waking him at midnight for more hours of practice" (p. 16).

Externally, this sort of overdevelopment of talent in an individual can be very impressive. But its effects on the psyche can be disastrous, especially for overachieving leaders who demand high volumes of unproductive work from themselves and those around them. Don't confuse the "busyness" this type of leader creates with the pursuit of excellence. They're not the same. In fact, these leaders are more likely to limit what others can offer. They have set the stage for dishonesty. A far-fetched example: If these types of leaders began walking around naked, their colleagues or subordinates might think twice about cluing them in. Some may withhold this information out of fear, others out of deference, and others because they no longer believe that insight is possible.

Competition and excellence: Are they really incompatible?

Peck (1993) coined the terms *pseudo consensus* and *adversarialism* to describe two ways that creative tension and real commitment are avoided in organizations. And David Whyte writes, "Work, paradoxically, does not ask enough of us, yet exhausts the narrow parts of us we do bring to its door" (2002, p. 22). Both authors are noting the overemphasis in the business world on short-term solutions and competition.

Some top business thinkers have gone so far as to state that competition and excellence are incompatible. This has been supported by recent findings in neuroscience. Neuroscientist Robert K. Cooper has noted that, on average, 25 to 40% of our work lives may be wasted or compromised due to an emphasis on competing (2001b). In addition, competition-fueled thinking often leads to less-than-optimal actions. He observes that "even thinking competitive thoughts can interfere with best performance and increase the release of negative stress hormones" (p. 29). Is your head spinning? Many small-circle high achievers are certainly scratching their heads. That's because they are rarely curious about themselves. In fact, competition directs their attention disproportionately to their interactions with the external world. They live as if they do not contribute to their own perspective, which they assume to be very close to objective reality.

Now we have a drama that is being consensually validated by the measure of success chosen, which serves only to reinforce and insulate all the constituencies. The boundaries of the smaller circle are secured by the daily pseudo-validation of who we define ourselves to be.

It sounds like an insurmountable problem, but don't give up. The paradox regarding competition and excellence can be resolved by looking at the relationship between the small and large circles. *Competition* is the process that occurs between two people or groups operating as small circles trying to gain an advantage over the other. *Pursuing excellence*, on the other hand, is the process of reducing the gap between the large and small circles. Ironically, the individuals and organizations that pursue excellence tend to have a competitive advantage over others. This is often an outcome of pursuing excellence, not a goal in itself.

In *Creating Competitive Advantage* (2006), bestselling business author Jaynie Smith says that competitive advantage is an outcome of self-awareness and the pursuit of excellence, not something imposed by power, vigilance, or brute force. Business leaders must be able to articulate why someone would choose their product over that of another company. On the other hand, leaders who have limited access to their own potential can disrupt the entire enterprise without realizing it. Even when a company seems to be doing well against its competitors, small-circle benchmarks are often being used to calibrate the success.

Peter Senge addresses this in *The Fifth Discipline* (2006), observing that benchmarking best practices can open people's eyes, but it can also do more harm than good. He states, "I do not believe great organizations have ever been built by trying to emulate another, any more than individual greatness is achieved by trying to copy another 'great person'" (p. 11).

It takes a true paradigm shift for leaders to become aware of their limitations.

Importantly, leaders' access to their larger selves is the upper limit of what they can achieve with others and the upper limit of their ability to build a genuine consensus to achieve the organization's vision. When the disparity between our functioning level (i.e., small circle) and our capability (i.e., large circle) is great, we tacitly limit what others in our organization can accomplish as well—even if, like us, they are capable of so much more.

A few startling quotes from Cooper are in order at this point:

> "Current performance and benchmarks, norms, and 'best practices' pale in comparison to individual and organizational capacity" (2001a).

> "Untapped human capacities amount to 90% to 97%. On average, less than 3% is applied effectively. The untapped 90% to 97% accounts for billions in revenue growth and cost savings." (2001a).

> "It has been reported that 50% to 85% of people believe they could double their productivity 'if they wanted to'…and they don't want to" (2001a).

These are startling statistics. Yet many businesses and corporations accept them as the cost of doing business. They couldn't be more wrong. These implicit costs are largely under the control of corporate leadership. It would take a true paradigm shift for leaders to become aware of their unrealized potential and begin to recapture lost energy and vision. It's worth it—business leaders who are committed to broadening access to their own potential by increasing their self-knowledge are in an optimal position to improve the quality and level of performance in their organization. This paradigm shift is so important in our knowledge-based business world. Knowledge is the product in our global playing field, and we increasingly need the full participation of all constituencies. And, although different cultures may define "success" somewhat differently, the qualities and values associated with great leadership appear to apply despite these differences and across time.

Responsible leaders can no longer afford the luxury of relative success. We must replace compliance with commitment, creativity, and innovation. Sustainable energy must become the fuel that propels an organization to continually evolve its capacity so that it can create its own future.

Next, we will look at a very powerful force that affects all living things and has the power to limit the success of individuals and companies at pursuing excellence.

What Have We Learned?

- Instead of being curious about our unrealized potential, we define ourselves as our knowable small circle. The rest of our energy is spent keeping our large circle outside our conscious awareness.

- Extremely high levels of achievement almost always come at the expense of other areas of the personality.

- When it comes to performance, the source of our motivation may be as important as the level of our motivation.

- While the display of overdeveloped individual talent can be impressive externally, the psychic effects can be disastrous.

- The boundaries of our small circle are reinforced by the daily pseudo-validation of who we define ourselves to be.

- Some top business thinkers believe that competition and excellence are incompatible. Competition is the process that occurs between two people or groups operating as small circles trying to gain an advantage over the other. Pursuing excellence is the process of reducing the gap between the circles.

- Leaders who have only limited access to their own potential can unknowingly disrupt the entire enterprise, but leaders who are committed to broadening access to their own potential through increasing their self-knowledge are in an optimal position to improve the quality and level of performance in their organization.

- Responsible leaders can no longer afford the luxury of relative success.

Understanding Resistance: How to Achieve Optimal Performance

Too much motivation can detract from performance to the same degree as too little. For a vast range of responsibilities and tasks, moderate levels of drive are tied to optimal performance.

Becoming the head of a large center of experienced psychologists and psychiatrists, many of whom probably felt they should have been offered the job, gave me quite an initiation to the subject of resistance. Though I had not sought the position, my appointment stirred up powerful conscious and unconscious feelings in my colleagues. Because my promotion was out of sync with general expectations, I immediately went to work, making sure that the members of the center's staff were recognized and rewarded whenever it was merited. But why did this work? It worked because of my seven-year-old self—I crafted a resolution to my early trauma (specifically, in regard to my parents) that contributed to a mental model that permitted me to absorb dissent and still support the sincere dissenter.

What I didn't fully realize at the time was how resistance as a force operates in work settings and how it tends to be activated when something threatens an important balance in our psyche. In a way, it is the psychological counterpart of the homeostatic mechanisms that regulate blood sugar levels, temperature, and other physiological processes. The real challenge lies in seeing how this resistance operates within ourselves.

Drive and ambition kept me from experiencing the calm energy that not only would have improved the quality of my performance but also would have liberated energy in my employees. This is why both too little drive and too much drive detract from optimal performance.[5] I was determined to resist acknowledging that I was subject to the same limitations and vulnerabilities as all human beings. It was not until years later that I learned about the value of moderation, particularly in terms of drive, for meaningful accomplishments in life and in work.

We've been talking about how we are all born with multiple abilities or potentials in a number of areas and how we all have the potential to excel if we're willing to explore our emotional and intellectual potential and seek

---

[5] The Yerkes-Dodson law (Yerkes & Dodson, 1908) represents the empirical relationship between drive or arousal and performance on a wide variety of tasks. The illustration on the facing page shows that optimal levels of performance (i.e., flow) are achieved at intermediate levels of arousal. Too little or too much arousal or drive is associated with weaker performance levels. Extreme levels of drive or arousal can result in negative physiological consequences or, in the extreme, impairment. Moderation is optimal for best performance.

YERKES-DODSON LAW

✦

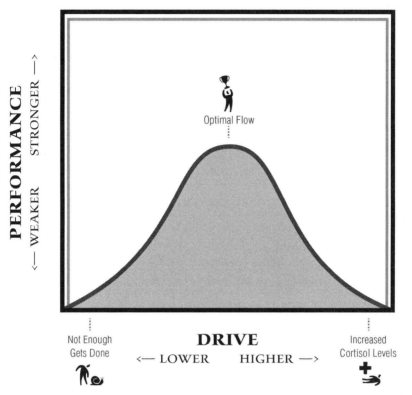

greater understanding. We have also posited that acquisition of inner knowledge influences the signals we emit, resulting in a tremendously positive impact on the people around us, including employees, coworkers, and family members. This path toward success has, however, another major roadblock—*resistance*.

What is resistance, and why is it such a roadblock?

Resistance is a force that opposes destabilization of an existing direction or balance. Here we are concerned with psychological resistance, which is an internal force that opposes efforts to bring repressed thoughts and feelings into consciousness. The clearest and most succinct description of resistance I have heard came from Margaret Wheatley, who described the concept simply and clearly: "Nothing living will obey. Even bacteria become penicillin resistant."

This illustrates our basic need for survival. Understanding emotional intelligence helps us break the code for emotional survival. Further, understanding how our minds work requires being able to distinguish harmful, interfering remnants from our species' past from helpful, protective remnants. Self-knowledge, an indispensable part of both processes, can help to make the expression of our need for emotional survival congruent with the operational and leadership practices we use. This is the key to unleashing great quantities of creativity and energy in our organizations.

Psychological resistance occurs in all of us. We all must compromise to align our natural propensities with the expectations of the external world. Once we develop an internal roadmap of how to best survive—and even thrive—we are reluctant to change it, even though it may objectively be in our best interest to do so. By their very nature, people want to be engaged. We all want to make meaningful contributions to our life and work. Yet, forces deep within our psyche can work at cross-purposes with these desires and thwart our best efforts. In some respects, forces and structures at work—control, hierarchy, defined duties, and responsibilities—seem to evoke resistance even in the best of circumstances. But they represent only precipitating causes that we are already predisposed to respond to based on prior learning. For example, compromises that result in avoiding commitment to accommodate a short-sighted, controlling parent (i.e., a predisposing cause) may be more likely to be evoked by a short-sighted, controlling boss (i.e., a precipitating cause). Most surprising, however, is that people are more likely to end up in the environment that recapitulates the characteristics of these early experiences because they seek an "at home" feeling, a place where they can be more comfortable. In some ways, this pattern affects all areas of our life, even in the best of circumstances. It is because of this pattern that doing the harder thing is the pathway to growth and change!

When we are children, we are motivated to maintain a safe relationship with our parents by assuming the role expected of us. This is the beginning of the division between the "ideal self" and the "true self." We banish our disowned parts to our unconscious, where they produce noise and disruption in our relationships throughout our lives. The more of our "true self" that is relegated to the unconscious, the greater the cost associated with the compromises we make. We internalize these compromises, and they become the unconscious or tacit mental models containing our beliefs about ourselves and others. In short, we live in the present but are governed by the past. Think of the overweight child who grows up to be thin but continues to see himself as fat. Early childhood experiences stick! In particular, unresolved parent-child issues lurk below the surface of our lives, stunting our effectiveness at work and in general. These models lead us to define ourselves as less than we are and frame our relationships with others on the basis of those definitions, influencing our senses and perceptions in unseen ways. They act as metaphorical lenses through which our interactions with the world are acted out in ways that preserve our beliefs.

This explains perfectly why we are so often blind to our own motivations and actions. Our mental models unconsciously influence what we see, and we interpret what we see as validation that our mental models represent reality. These models govern all our transactions and interactions, ensuring that our definitions of ourselves remain "small-circle." But something else keeps many of us from taking action to break out of the pattern: Fear.

How do fear and resistance manifest?

Internal emotional states of resistance include feelings of invisibility, powerlessness, anxiety, lethargy, boredom, unmotivation, and anger. In the workplace, employee resistance may be expressed by poor performance, extended lunch breaks, deception, or eye-rolling behind the boss's back. The "unseen" expressions of resistance—in the employee's relationship to his or her bosses, coworkers, and authority figures—are probably the most revealing, as they're a statement of the worker's limited access to him- or herself and a lack of desire to offer his or her best at work. These are simply the thoughts, emotions, and behaviors linked to our internal mental models and associated with early compromises in our life that keep us from being our best. They can take many forms, including fear, worry and risk avoidance, and a readiness to expect punishment. In essence, resistance in the workplace primarily keeps employees from knowing what they fear about themselves. Becoming aware of these unconscious parts of ourselves is often frightening—but it's also the typical subjective experience associated with this type of discovery.

By looking at the extent to which we encounter these and other forms of resistance from others, we can get a good idea of our own level of self-knowledge. It is especially telling if we encounter resistance with noticeable consistency from multiple people at work and in other environments; for example, if we rarely hear bad news or our ideas are rarely challenged or even commented on by anyone in the organization. These patterns are developed early in life, even in the absence of major trauma. Subsequent experience validates and reinforces our self-image to ourselves and to others.

This presents an interesting paradox. The frontal lobes are the executive center of our brains. While they can be hijacked by the emotional centers deep within our brains, they also have the capacity to inhibit the unrestrained thoughts and behaviors that can occur in response to threat. But the circuitry associated with the modulation of unrestrained emotional reactions to threat does not fully mature until our mid-twenties. This is in part why our early mental models are not always the best guides to get us through the trajectory of life. Once our frontal lobes mature, however, some important things become possible. We develop the capacity to override the prior learning habits that have limited us, broadening our access to others. This presents us an opportunity to develop higher-level defenses.

Imagine taking a walk through almost any shopping mall. You'll encounter many different types of people, all with different mental models and belief systems and all wrapped up in their own unique experiences at that moment. Some will be friendly, others will be preoccupied—maybe glued to their cell phones—some will look at us, and others will look away. Assuming they are even aware of us, their response to us is in part a reflection of their experience and our social impact on others. Now, imagine a naked but calm man walking through the same mall, encountering those same people. He will not receive the same differentiated responses that you did. Instead, virtually everyone will respond in a similar manner—they will become hyper-vigilant, move away, and create a safe boundary for themselves. Rarely will someone actually approach him.

This principle might be stated as such: Our estrangement from our true selves affects what we communicate to others and how they respond to us, and fortifies our existing belief system about ourselves and the world. If you find yourself being wary of, disappointed with, or uncomfortable with others, consider the possibility that you may be contributing to the very behaviors in others that are causing you discomfort.

Change is difficult because our belief system reinforces our experiences, and vice-versa.

Now you can begin to appreciate why change is so difficult. For instance, the naked man, who is probably psychotic, is unlikely to think "Of course people are moving away; I am naked and scaring them." More likely, he has some internal narrative that explains the behavior of others in a different way, like "I am so important and powerful that others move away because they fear my greatness." The connection is easy to see in this extreme example, but much more difficult to see in the more conventional situations most of us encounter on a day-to-day basis.

The less we know ourselves, the more likely it is that we will be unaware of the impact we have on others. People who live their lives as very small circles live in a less differentiated world. Although they may feel that they're in control, they cannot rid themselves of the feeling that the rapture of being fully alive is eluding them. Because they don't know themselves as well as they could, their rules for living must come from the outside.

Consider the case of a bright, capable CEO running a major corporation in an economy in which knowledge creation is critical and social media is ready to immediately advertise every misstep to the world. This executive will not be effective, especially during periods of high stress, if he relies on mental models developed early in life because these models will not represent what is possible for him or for those whose lives he affects. In his effort to move things along, he may actually slow them down because his mental models won't allow him to be flexible when it is most needed. His response…ability will be compromised at the most critical moments.

Consider too the case of a business leader who, during an annual review, gave an employee several suggestions for improvement. At the first hint of critique, the employee burst out crying and said, "You are just like my mother!" Even though the suggestion for improvement was addressed mildly, the employee overreacted, showing just how much our early life models can affect our adult life—in this case, negatively.

The limiting power of our unexamined selves is especially potent when we're at the top.

If we are in a position of control, power issues may complicate the picture even further. In 2011, David Kirkpatrick summed it up in a *Forbes* article as follows: "In this new world of business, companies and leaders will have to show authenticity, fairness, transparency and good faith. If they don't, customers and employees may come to distrust them, to potentially disastrous effect."

In our knowledge-based global economy, every person must be at his or her creative best just to keep the organization competitive. But will they feel free to create, make mistakes, and contribute to an energetic atmosphere that supports self-awareness in the service of innovation? Kirkpatrick underscores why this new social contract cannot be ignored or sidestepped: "Newly armed customer and employee activists can become the source of creativity, innovation and new ideas to take your company forward." This point is further emphasized by longtime Harvard Business School professor Shoshana Zuboff, quoted within the article: "…in this new world value is not created inside the organization. It rests in the unfulfilled needs and desires of the individual."

How does resistance affect daily functioning?

Resistance is something that can stop your effort dead in its tracks and can create unseen consequences for you and your company. In fact, it may be the biggest problem you encounter. Let's summarize the main points about resistance and how it affects daily function.

- Unexamined mental models, which operate outside of our conscious awareness, limit optimal access to our true selves so that our functional ability is less than our innate ability. Mental models limit how we experience ourselves and what we can see in ourselves and others.

- Mental models bias our perception, making us feel more comfortable with situations and experiences that reinforce our unconscious beliefs and giving greater weight to choices that validate our early compromises. When we do not feel comfortable, the forces of resistance become activated, and it takes great resolve not to yield to them.

- Psychological resistance is the interface between tacit mental models and the external world. Although designed for self-preservation, it often protects outdated compromises, which were appropriate to earlier situations as interpreted by an immature brain.

- Resistance in the workplace is often unintentional (i.e., the source is unconscious) and represents both a great cost and a great opportunity for gaining competitive advantage in the business world, particularly when knowledge is the product.

- Resistance is costly for at least two reasons: first, it detracts from energy that you could direct toward excellence—it requires energy to keep something hidden from yourself—and second, it restricts the range of thoughts and emotions that others feel comfortable sharing with you— even unconsciously—and thus the talents they will apply to their work.

Self-knowledge is not an easy path, but the rewards are great for both individuals and organizations. And if this path starts at the top of the chain (i.e., the executive level), the results can be incredible.

Next we'll take a very general look at what happens inside our brains. This will help us understand how we get in our own way and how we can begin to change our own biochemistry.

──────What Have We Learned?──────

- Resistance is a survival mechanism we use to preserve ourselves physiologically and psychologically.

- All of us adapt to microcosms of the world by making compromises that often limit access to our true potential. The more of our true self that is relegated to the unconscious, the greater the cost associated with the compromises. The less we know ourselves, the more likely we will be unaware of the impact we have on others.

- There are some internal states that may indicate resistance and several ways employee resistance can manifest, but unseen expressions of resistance may be the most damaging of all.

- Once our frontal lobes mature, we have the capacity to override prior learning that limits us, broadening our access to others.

- In our knowledge-based global economy, each person must be at his or her creative best just to keep the organization competitive.

- Resistance in the workplace is often unintentional and represents both a great cost and a great opportunity for gaining competitive advantage in the business world.

- Objective self-knowledge gained through the process of self-discovery changes our mental models and aligns them more closely with reality.

Changing Expectations Changes Possibilities:
The Neuroscience of Leadership

Doing the harder thing can change self-limiting mental models. It can make you aware of roadblocks that keep you from knowing and pursuing your biggest dreams.

The cerebral cortex…doesn't simply learn; it is always learning to learn.

Neurons that fire together wire together.

Norman Doidge, 2007

Like most of ours, my pattern of relating to internal and external constituencies at work and at home had been established in early life and well-rehearsed. Every decision, interaction, and action reinforced this early template and strengthened the brain circuitry surrounding it. In life, we generally negotiate the world as best we can guided by mental models that we constructed to make sense of childhood experiences—experiences that occurred when we were too young to see the bigger picture of our lives. If we make sense of things by cutting off too much of our potential—in essence, by selling ourselves short—our body and/or mind is equipped to create "symptoms" like boredom, detachment, substance abuse, anxiety, depression, and anger to fill the gap. These can keep us from experiencing both the joys of success and the rapture of being fully alive. For me, these symptoms were fear and anxiety. I didn't experience these emotions consciously (remember, I was invulnerable), but they significantly influenced the high level of drive I directed toward mastery of the external world. And my high level of drive kept me too busy to reflect on what was occurring deep inside.

Sometimes it is not until many years later that you fully recognize or appreciate one of life's unexpected gifts. My father, a bright and gentle soul, must have realized that, even when I was an adolescent, too much of my ambition was driven by anticipatory anxiety and too little of it directed toward meaningful and satisfying accomplishment. Characteristically, he brought an audio presentation of relaxation exercises home one evening and asked me to share my opinion of it with him. After ignoring his request for a couple of weeks, I decided to listen to it one boring afternoon when no was else was home. To my amazement, the exercises on the tape enabled me to experience a level of relaxation and calm that I didn't think was possible. (Even our resting tension level is linked to the early circuits that represent the biological bases of our mental models.)

The most important lesson learned here had nothing to do with finally acquiescing to my father's wishes, the tension reduction exercises themselves, or the profound level of relaxation and psychic calm I experienced. It was the *disconfirmation* of my belief that my base level of tension was unchangeable. As a consequence, my well-fortified mental model of the world was fractured; I would never be able to reconstruct it in quite the same way again. This simple, one-time experience was the seed for later spiritual and psychological growth, but I didn't know it at the time. Curiously, I never repeated the exercises, though the feeling of calm and relaxation it induced was quite pleasurable. I know now that I was a long way from facing my demons—but the clock was now ticking.

Now that we have opened up a Pandora's box filled with resistance, it's easier to see just what a roadblock it is and how it can instill bad habits in us. Psychological resistance exerts a force that pulls us toward the pathways we have taken in the past. This force is in opposition to the positive force that pushes us to acknowledge more of our large-circle potential. There are parts of each of us that resist change, both internally and externally.

Ironically, it's the very external changes—the ones we are most likely to resist—that have the most potential to stretch us toward our greater selves. The strength of this force is augmented by neurobiological changes in the brain that encode both our experiences and the ways we adapt to them. There is little question that the relationship between the brain and our culture is reciprocal: Our brain shapes our culture and our culture shapes our brain. Virtually every sustained activity changes the brain, and cultural activities are no exception. According to behavioral psychologist Donald O. Hebb and neuroplasticity expert Michael Merzenich, our brains are most likely substantially changed both physically and functionally each time we learn a new skill (Doidge, 2007).

A little "brain education" is now in order.

The culture we've experienced through our family and other groups may actually determine what we perceive. For many of us, that's a hard pill to swallow; we tend to feel that we are the masters of our own behaviors and beliefs. But if you think about it, you'll begin to realize just how much culture affects us. Our expectations of others, our rate of speech, our propensity to misinterpret the motivation of others—these are all examples of how our view of everything can be shaped by culture. It becomes clear that what causes a behavior is just as important as the behavior itself. This is true even if the behavior was based on early mental models but resulted in positive outcomes. After the neurological structures that sustain our functional ability are put into practice and, eventually, become the basis for our sensory and perceptual habits and beliefs (i.e., mental models), we find it very difficult to change. The neuronal connections responsible for what appears to be the same behavior on repeated occasions are actually slightly different each time because of intervening material—thoughts have occurred to us, we have taken various actions. Nevertheless, the experiences are similar enough to create a strong habit that guides us to respond to situations in similar ways.

The brain also protects established habits by screening the information that it allows into the system. Cooper (2001b) observed that structures in our brain stem actually review information en route to our brain from our cranial nerves and give the highest priority to messages conveying the concept of *danger*—even those conveying the possibility of it. In the face of ambiguity, we resort to familiar habits. Our brain signals the alarm, frames the danger based on our primitive decision rules, and compels us to take action based on habits established from prior experience. So, although both tendencies (i.e., we interpret ambiguity as danger, we respond habitually with greater intensity) are hardwired, the familiar pathways are written and overwritten on our neurobiology, strengthening the sensory and perceptual habits that sustain our mental models of both ourselves and the world around us.

Let's speculate about why these tendencies are hardwired into our brains. Our distant ancestors no doubt lived under conditions of extreme physical danger. Those who survived to live another day and contribute to their offspring's survival were probably more effective at detecting and responding to danger than those who didn't survive. Their success eventually became hardwired. Now, jump ahead in time to us, their descendants. This wiring can actually work against us because we face an entirely different set of dangers. Most of the dangers we confront tend to involve social-evaluative threats as opposed to potential physical harm. In our social-evaluative world, hasty actions often gratify primitive urges but rarely lead to effective solutions.

How do we go about making real changes?

A new question arises. With family, culture, belief systems, mental models, and now neurobiology sustaining our habits and predispositions, is it even possible to make real change? "Yes, according to [Alvaro] Pascual-Leone [chief of the Harvard Medical School center for magnetic brain stimulation], but it is difficult because, once we have created these tracks, they become 'really speedy' and very efficient…To take a different path becomes increasingly difficult. A roadblock of some kind is necessary to help us change direction" (Doidge, 2007, p. 209).

The genuine pursuit of self-knowledge leads us to stimulate and develop areas of our brain (i.e., the prefrontal cortex) that have the capacity to override prior learning (see Appendix A for a list of activities that can lead to frontal lobe stimulation). This often requires us to do the harder thing when it appears to be the best alternative, even if it is less gratifying than the consciously favored hardwired actions. But can we create roadblocks that encourage us to rewire our brains and are disruptive enough to encourage positive change while managing the temptation to rely on stagnating habits that have outlived their adaptive value to us?

To know the answer to this, we must understand the physiology of our brains, starting with our frontal lobes. The frontal lobes are the executive center of our mind/body, where selective information from the body and brain (which are not really separate) converge. This is where we make conscious choices. But, importantly, the information used to make these choices is limited to what our tacit mental models and biological substrate have allowed to get there in the first place.

Candace Pert, who lectures on how our thoughts and feelings influence our health and well-being, makes a similar point. In her book about the relationship between human physiology, emotions, and consciousness (1999), Pert reveals how our emotions transform our bodies and create our state of health through their relationship with cells, molecules, and peptides. In her words, "consciousness creates reality" (p. 250); she observes that the cost of choosing to live within a tiny percentage (i.e., small circle) of our dynamic range of expressivity can be a costly mistake.

Succinctly, she reminds us that "there is no state of mind that is not mimicked by the immune system" (2004). In other words, through knowledge, understanding, and self-discovery, business leaders can begin to face their own functional and biological roadblocks, learning how their minds work to preserve what they believe at the expense of their effectiveness and perhaps their health. Self-knowledge, including awareness of our habitual responses, opens us to the possibility of trying new things, in turn increasing the options available to us. As the comfort and familiarity of old habits gradually lose their hold, we have an opportunity to grow in the direction of our large circle. In essence, the cost-benefit of "doing the harder thing" shifts in the positive direction.

The human brain is remarkably malleable.

It's important to note that, because this process involves engagement of the prefrontal cortex of our brains, we are not likely to derive full advantage prior to brain development that occurs in about our mid-twenties. This fact is a game-changer. For many years it was thought that our capacity to learn new patterns reached its height in our mid-twenties and declined steadily after that. New research is now revealing a great deal of evidence that the human brain is capable of changing itself throughout life. We now know that our thoughts and emotions can actually change the structure and function of the brain itself.

In his book *The Brain That Changes Itself* (2007), Norman Doidge cites Nobel Laureate Gerald Edelman, who substantiated the remarkable abilities of the human brain. Edelman observed that "the human cortex alone has 30 billion neurons and is capable of making 1 million billion synaptic connections" (p. 294). This means that there are "10 followed by at least a million zeros" of potential neural circuits, and "10 followed by 79 zeros, give or take a few, of particles in the known universe." Doidge concludes: "These staggering numbers explain why the human brain can be described as the most complex known object in the universe." It's difficult to wrap your arms around that one!

There are many other fascinating examples of the brain changing significantly, from primate studies to astonishing changes in people whose lives have been positively transformed. One of many examples presented by Doidge (2007) is based on a series of brain mapping studies conducted by Merzenich. In one experiment, he was able to show that five separate brain maps corresponding to each of a monkey's five fingers changed into four when two of the primate's fingers were sewn together for several months. The neurons that used to fire separately now fired simultaneously, becoming wired together. This and other brilliant studies presented in Doidge's book illustrate that change is not only possible but happening frequently, especially in cases in which the options to preserve the status quo involve more work than what would be required by change.

That is precisely the kind of bind that the striving for growth creates within us, helping to encourage us to move in the direction of our potential. Everyone can eventually get there—the question is, will it be kicking and screaming or voluntarily and serenely? The choice you make in that moment, and in the many other opportunities for growth presented throughout life, will define your life.

M. Scott Peck expressed this beautifully when he described the process of enlarging our lives. "The unconscious is always one step ahead of the conscious mind in either the right or wrong direction. It is therefore impossible ever to know that what you are doing is right, since knowing is a function of consciousness. However, if your will is steadfastly to the good, and you are willing to suffer fully when the good seems ambiguous (which, to me, is about ninety-eight percent of the time), then your unconscious will be always be one step ahead of your conscious mind in the right direction. In other words, the Holy Spirit will lead you and you will do the right thing. Only you won't have the luxury of knowing it at the time you're doing it. Indeed, you will do the right thing precisely because you have been willing to forgo that luxury" (1983, p. 91).

Beware: You might crash without self-knowledge.

Leading a business without self-knowledge is like flying an airplane without all the instruments visible. The potential allowed by the design and components cannot be fully realized because critical information is not available in the cockpit (i.e., the plane's frontal lobes). Of course, it may be possible to continue flying if the conditions are favorable and certain important gauges are working, but it's risky. Some "good-to-great" companies that no longer exist were able to do this impressively for some time before they crashed.

Many of us pilot complex equipment (i.e., our large circles) relying on visual flight rules alone (i.e., our small circles). There is no substitute for fluid access to all the equipment (using gauges that are accurately calibrated and operational, of course) if we want to get to our destination in a safe and efficient manner. However, if our operating out of small circles is not always obvious to us and there are all sorts of forces aligned to keep our circles small, how do we become aware of the hidden costs imposed on our lives and our leadership effectiveness?

To answer this question, it will be helpful to reexamine the area of the brain that makes us distinctly human: the frontal cortex. You'll recall that the frontal cortex may be thought of as the executive center of the brain, where choices are made based on information that arrives there and enters into consciousness. It appears that a function of the frontal cortex is to decide where our mind should focus; as a consequence, it has the potential to affect other parts of the brain. An example: Evidence shows that even one humiliation in childhood can permanently alter the amygdale[6]—but even this permanent alteration can be overridden by engagement of areas of the left prefrontal cortex.

Even with all the fortifications supporting our small circles and the accompanying screening of disconfirming information, most of us with an intact frontal cortex are able to revise self-limiting prior learning. But information enters the brain from receptors all over the body, and only a portion (usually, too little) actually reaches the frontal cortex. So, we see the same pattern: Our early mental models and psychological defenses help to preserve our early beliefs, even when they are serving only to hold us back from our unrealized potential.

We have already learned that the brain prioritizes danger messages and that prior learning (i.e., mental models) supported by neurological hardware can filter out information that would create a disruption to our belief system. How do we begin to activate our dormant instruments and recalibrate the accompanying gauges to take full advantage of our equipment and design in the service of growing our business?

Our internal sense of well-being can actually serve as a good gauge of progress, since our brains may be designed to experience positive feeling when we are open to experience at the psychological, spiritual, and biochemical levels, all of which are linked to one another. Although there is a lot of variation in humans, high concentrations of endorphin receptors, many of which are located in the frontal cortex, appear to produce pleasurable feelings. This seems to indicate that when our frontal lobes are engaged, we may feel quite good. We can thank God for that one!

Realistically, changing your mental models by doing the harder thing may initially generate anxiety, which is anything but enjoyable. Nevertheless, many who have successfully confronted this type of fear know a distinctive feeling of satisfaction and well-being. (It is interesting to note that, from an evolutionary perspective, the "anxiety peptide" is relatively new. In the words

---

[6] The amygdale is located in the center of the brain and functions as the brain's sentinel. After giving priority to danger signals, the amygdale responds to sensory input like a hair trigger that has the capability of hijacking the rest of the brain. It is only after the pathways between the amygdale and the left prefrontal area of the brain mature (during our mid-twenties) that we can inhibit and ultimately refine the amygdale's ability to add value to our decisions. We are then in a position to understand what our emotions are telling us and enlarge our capacity to know how our mind works.

of Pert [2004], "It's a sign that you have enough cortical matter to visualize two or three choices and experience conflict about which one to choose.")

In many respects, we are designed to succeed and, like instrumentation in a cockpit, our bodies uniquely inform us—through boredom, anxiety, and euphoria—when we're on our flight path and when we're off course. When there is no potential for growth, we experience boredom. When we are about to take on a challenge or do the harder thing, we experience anxiety. When we have changed our mental models and expanded our level of self-knowledge, we experience feelings of satisfaction, well-being, and sometimes euphoria.

Now that we know that we can change in unimagined ways, let's delve deeper into leadership, self-knowledge, and the kind of change that can set us apart from others. In the next chapter, we'll take a look at how organizational and cultural design can actually support and encourage personal mastery and fundamental learning in the service of individual and corporate success.

What Have We Learned?

- Our brain shapes our culture and our culture shapes our brain.

- We have two hardwired tendencies: We exhibit a habit strength that guides our readiness to respond to perceived situations in similar ways, and the brain protects established habits by screening the information that it allows into the system.

- The genuine pursuit of self-knowledge leads us to stimulate and develop areas of our brain (i.e., the frontal cortex) that have the capacity to override prior learning.

- Through knowledge, understanding, and self-discovery, business leaders can begin to face their own functional and biological roadblocks.

- The human brain is capable of changing itself throughout life. Most of us with an intact frontal cortex are able to revise self-limiting prior learning.

- In many respects we are designed to succeed and our bodies uniquely inform us—through boredom, anxiety, and euphoria—where we are on our flight path and when we might be off course.

The Optimal Organization: Liberating Productive Energy Through Alignment of Purpose

There are basic disciplines that must be mastered for creating sustainable, evolving organizational effectiveness. How these are addressed and energized is largely dependent on the leader's level of self-knowledge. The self-aware leader knows he or she is part of a system and that his or her level of personal mastery sets a limit on what can be achieved by the organization.

In the second decade of my university career I was fortunate to be part of a group of very smart, upper-level leaders who met monthly to talk about the application of cutting-edge ideas to our institution's evolution. We read and talked about hundreds of books (mostly business-related) that influenced and expanded my ideas about how to create optimal organizations. Already knowledgeable in the subject of human functioning, I also had a good intellectual understanding about how to help people develop greater effectiveness through personal mastery. These meaningful conversations with my peers helped me to see how my knowledge base could be put to better use. By looking at our organization as a dynamic and evolving system, I was better able to see how energy and creativity could be liberated and how to invigorate myself and others in a way that had previously eluded me. There was still more to be done, but I had moved forward.

It was at this point that I read Peter Senge's *The Fifth Discipline*. The first 100 pages were enough to show me that this was a groundbreaking work. I was filled with excitement when I realized that Senge had integrated knowledge about how people function with ideas about potential for organizations. Each person in the organization has a responsibility to develop him- or herself, be honest and open with his or her teams and groups, participate in the creation of a worthy vision, and accept his or her profound responsibility to the larger purpose. This was music to my ears; Senge's words helped me apply what I knew about people to his view that organizations can learn and that organizational learning is dependent on what those within it accomplish for themselves and each other.

I could see for myself a role in co-creating an optimal system for producing great work. My job now was to create an organization that was capable of learning and evolving on its own. This could be accomplished only if those attached to the enterprise acknowledged their interdependency with others in the organization, including the customer base.

Intellectually, I began to realize that my focus must shift from steering the ship to designing the ship. Here was an opportunity to create an organization that was dynamic and could learn, an organization in which everyone took ownership for the vision and each person was committed to his or her self-development and was willing to offer his or her best thoughts and ideas without fear. Though it was an anxious transition, this shift brought me great relief.

Seeing the organization transform itself before my eyes and recognizing the abundance that had been there all along was a grander version of the relaxation tape experience. Ultimately, it was also the impetus behind my need to learn how my mind worked and to liberate my passion to transform myself and others.

In *Emotional Intelligence* (2005), Daniel Goleman tells the story of Captain McBroom, an airline pilot who, during a flight, was so focused on a landing gear problem that he failed to notice he was running out of fuel. But this was not the problem. The problem was that Captain McBroom's crew members had noticed the low fuel gauges but were afraid to clue him in. The captain had created a culture in the cockpit that made bringing this critical life-saving information to his attention all but impossible. Ten people lost their lives in the crash that ensued. Goleman observed that "In 80 percent of airline crashes, pilots make mistakes that could have been prevented, particularly if the crew worked together more harmoniously" (p. 148). Captain McBroom's connection to others was an extension of his own level of self-awareness.

This is relevant because "the cockpit is a microcosm of any working organization" (Goleman, 2005, p. 148). The destructive effects of misery, intimidation, and low morale contributed to by arrogant, non-self-aware bosses can go largely unnoticed for very long periods of time. The costs of these effects can be temporarily disguised by "relative success," but eventually lower productivity, poor morale, missed deadlines, and increased errors occur as the organization loses its competitive advantage and employees leave the organization for more congenial, growth-enhancing settings. As Goleman observes, "There is, inevitably, a cost to the bottom line from low levels of emotional intelligence on the job" (p. 148).

CEO self-knowledge is a necessary condition for building a genuine consensus to achieve a vision: A recap.

We've identified the qualities and values of great leaders in history and shown that these tenets are as relevant today as they were in the past. They continue to be qualities that contribute to our optimal ability to work together. We also identified our greatest sin or shortcoming as hubris, which was defined as the abuse of the powerless by those in power. Hubris can be thought of as arrogance or malignant narcissism and is in total contrast with humility, which may be thought of as "knowing yourself as you truly are." To oversimplify, humility is a cognitive and emotional state that accompanies self-knowledge, whereas hubris is a way of running away from the disowned parts of ourselves, an exertion of some form of unwelcome control over people and situations that threaten to expose our true selves. Very few exceptions exist. We went on to explore how we are all required to compromise access to our natural endowment and construct mental models that often overdevelop parts of us at the expense of other parts. We explored how these mental models affect business response...ability; when combined with institutional power, they can actually determine what others experience and are willing to offer. We also looked at the concept of resistance as a pervasive tendency that is fortified by hardwired neurological tendencies, psychological habits, and biochemical pathways linked to emotional states. In addition, we identified some things we can do to begin unraveling this limiting network in the interest of expanding our access to ourselves.

We are now in a position to address the following question, whose answer should not be taken lightly because it has enormous implications for the future of any organization:

> How can a CEO facilitate a culture within his or her
> organization that supports optimal development of its
> constituents and guides creative energies toward
> innovation, knowledge creation, excellence, and
> competitive advantage?

The optimal organization in the twenty-first century is the learning organization. Peter Senge's classic *The Fifth Discipline*, the introduction of this concept to the business world, focuses on the art and practice of the learning organization. This work and the many that followed represent a major leap forward in creating organizational effectiveness and desired futures. It addresses the major domains of human functioning that must be understood and mastered in order to create a dynamic and evolving business.

How do we start building learning organizations?
The concept of a learning organization requires an architecture that reflects principal interdependent components that must be mastered to be optimally

effective in knowledge creation. When top leadership has acquired self-knowledge, the chances of optimal effectiveness are increased because leadership clearly understands how best to create the desired future.

The Fifth Discipline (2006) looked at organizations as dynamic creations of the humans functioning within it—in which CEO awareness could be conceptualized as a multiplier of ability and power. CEO self-knowledge creates greater clarity throughout the organization because the CEO has learned how his or her own mind works and can apply the same process to helping others create the same understanding. Once those at the top level of leadership are attuned to their own systemic structure, the extension of their inner knowledge to systems within the organization becomes much clearer. As a consequence, the CEO relates to constituents with greater objectivity and emotional intelligence. When leadership changes in this way, the chances for positive growth throughout the organization are optimized, and, simultaneously, leadership offers a model for direct reports to emulate in relating to their own coworkers and supervisees. Senge describes organizations that will truly excel in the future as those that discover how to tap people's commitment and capacity to learn at all levels of the organization.

This change has to start at the top because, like school, work recapitulates the framework of prior learning begun in childhood. In this context, compromise formations, mental models, and modeling are variables that are simply too powerful to ignore. A leader's excitement at expanding his or her concept of excellence through self-discovery will model possibilities for others and provide a milieu that increases the likelihood of all people within the organization being able to evolve their capacity. Commitment is a function of the possibility of growth. This is a truth you can take to the bank! Just think about any relationship in which there is no potential for growth. Commitment wanes, and energy is directed elsewhere. The same thing happens in companies.

In the introduction to the revised and updated edition of *The Fifth Discipline* (2006), Senge presents some core ideas that have profound implications for the importance of self-knowledge, especially at the top of organizations:

> "There are ways of working together that are vastly
> more satisfying and more productive than the
> prevailing system of management" (p. xviii).

> "Organizations work the way they do because of how we work, how we think and interact; the changes required ahead are not only in our organizations but in ourselves as well" (p. xviii).

> "In building learning organizations there is no ultimate destination or end state, only a lifelong journey" (p. xviii).

In his summary, Senge concludes,

> I believe that, the prevailing system of management is, at its core, dedicated to mediocrity. It forces people to work harder and harder to compensate for failing to tap the spirit and collective intelligence that characterizes working together at their best. (p. xviii)

Organizational learning disabilities diminish potential.

Senge (2006) goes on to present several organizational "learning disabilities" that represent departures from reality and excellence. These are ways that businesses and organizations avoid transformational learning and, as a result, actually erode their individual and collective potential. My two favorites are "the illusion of taking charge" (not seeing how we contribute to our own problems; p. 20), and "the delusion of learning from experience" (experience is a great teacher but we rarely directly experience the consequences of our most important decisions; p. 23).

We can learn three great lessons here about organizational learning disabilities:

1. Structure influences behavior.

2. Structure in human systems is subtle.

3. Leverage often comes from new ways of thinking.

The first two speak to the gravity of systems for both good and bad outcomes, and the third addresses how changes in perspective can influence the direction of outcomes.

A learning organization continually evolves its capacity to create its own future. It embraces the dynamic interplay between aspiration, self-discovery, self-mastery, emotional intelligence, and systemic functioning. In *The Fifth Discipline*, Senge identifies five disciplines that must be mastered in order to create a learning organization:

- **Shared vision**: A purpose worthy of believing in.

- **Personal mastery**: Self-discovery and self-knowledge.

- **Mental models**: Psychological lenses that influence access to ourselves and others.

- **Team learning**: Exercising curiosity about self and others through open dialogue.

- **Systems thinking**: The dynamic network created by interrelated actions in organizations that represents the foundation of the disciplines.

To expound slightly on the last of these, in systems thinking, every influence is both cause and effect. We all contribute and influence our reality on a relatively continuous basis.

Mastery of each of these disciplines is predicated on a level of interpersonal effectiveness that is born of self-knowledge. Self-knowledge is a key that unlocks many doors, yet it has remained a mostly elusive concept in much of the business literature, which assumes that what is inside us is a given while focusing on how to master what is outside. Understanding the importance of this is critical to business for the knowledge worker of the twenty-first century.

Our bodies are a good example. Healthy bodies promote life through stability. But optimal bodies are regularly destabilized (e.g., through exercise) in the short run to promote greater fitness in the long run. Likewise, in the acquisition of self-knowledge, homeostatic processes are called into play, representing a kind of organizational force, which, when combined with individual resistance, work against growth and change by opting for what we already know. In many respects, "all things change when we do" (Whyte, 2002, p. 93). "Individuals committed to a vision beyond their [unenlightened] self-interest find they have energy not available when pursuing narrower goals, as will organizations that tap this level of commitment" (Senge, 2006, p. 161). Just as calm energy and positive feelings signal that the frontal lobes are being stimulated, the level of morale in an organization is a measure of how much organizational intelligence is being accessed and put to use. Sophisticated coaching focuses on removing individual limitations on growth and awareness. Dynamic cultural change in organizations requires a self-aware leader who is focused on addressing limits on growth in his or her company.

Sometimes, it is better to do nothing than to choose the solution that provides short-term results.

The unaware leader faces a great danger in that he or she will be tempted by symptomatic solutions that appear to offer a successful resolution in the short run. When this is the case, it may be better to do nothing. When nothing is attempted, underlying systemic issues will, at the very least, continue to produce warning signs that are increasingly difficult to ignore. Palliative fixes, on the other hand, may create the illusion that the problem has been addressed when it has merely been postponed. For example, the U.S. continually deals with a budget crisis. Congress "kicks the can" down the road while our economy becomes more and more damaged. The lack of a leader or leaders who can rally members of Congress to engage in the proper behavior to energetically and creatively approach the problem is going to have negative, long-lasting effects on our country. This concept is beautifully summarized by Senge (2006): "Our non-systemic ways of thinking consistently lead us to focus on low-leverage changes. Because we don't see the structures underlying our actions, we focus on symptoms where the stress is greatest" (p. 113).[7]

While this tendency can be attributed to information overload and excessive work demands, the fact is that we can see on the outside only what we can access on the inside. In other words, our relationship with ourselves can be based on illusions (i.e., early models) or dedicated to reality at all costs. Problematic is that the unaware person often enjoys a greater level of certainty than the more self-aware and enlightened. Take, for example, the CEO of a large publicly traded company who frequently intruded on critical sales meetings with important customers to insure that nothing important was left unsaid. In his haste to make the deal, he undermined the system. The information he imparted was accurate and, under different circumstances, might have been welcomed. But his method communicated disrespect for the

---

[7] These structures become evident as our metaphorical lenses are replaced by clearer glass.

salesperson and the customer. In fact, he was tacitly weakening the credibility of the salesperson by inadvertently raising questions about the information that had already been presented. Almost certainly, the salesperson experienced a negative emotional reaction that, given the power differential between the two, likely remained unexpressed. The CEO's behavior eroded the systemic structure of the organization, though he remained unaware of the negative consequences to morale, commitment, confidence, and customer loyalty. In this type of situation, the ramifications are, in fact, worse if the customer decides to make the purchase despite his shaken confidence in the product and company than if the sale is lost, because the consequences of this and similar actions would remain dormant yet still powerful enough to diminish the organization's effectiveness over time. In this case, the CEO had years of exemplary sales experience and a stellar record to back it up. Clearly, he had a lot to offer both the customer and the sales force. But his mental models of himself and others led him to exert too much control—he should have either stayed away or participated as a passive observer. We cannot apprehend the systemic structure of organizations if we are blind to our mental models, which frequently focus our attention on the wrong events.

Senge observed that few are trained to see systematic details and dynamic complexity. The importance of psychological training and skill in helping business leaders acquire this level of insight and clarity cannot be overstated. Learning, as defined in *The Fifth Discipline*, is "changing your mental models." This kind of learning is generally achieved by psychotherapy or psychoanalysis, both of which require significant investments of commitment, time, and money.

The most effective way of furthering self-discovery and self-knowledge in a business context is probably through executive coaching. But a "coach" can be anyone, from someone who is currently out of work to a highly trained and experienced psychologist who is an expert at these very transformations. There are simply too few trained coaches, psychologists, and consultants who combine business knowledge with an in-depth understanding of human functioning.

One of the goals of CEO Effectiveness, LLC is to develop a list of highly trained and credentialed professionals who know how to create the transformational change that helps business leaders and businesses continually evolve their own capacity to create and maintain competitive advantage. It is also dedicated to encouraging this transformation by helping business leaders focus on the point of greatest leverage and offering a gradation of information and experiences to all whose "pilot light" still flickers. What we are blind to in ourselves we are unable to see in others, and the cost of our blindness to individuals, organizations, and society is great.

A major purpose of this brief work and our company is to help business leaders begin this transformation by introducing them to information that illustrates both the business and personal advantages of the journey to self-knowledge, an adventure that is closely linked to spiritual growth.

The alternative to personal growth is not stagnation, it's deterioration.

We are designed as dynamic systems and are therefore incapable of furthering larger dynamic systems (e.g., companies, families) if we lack the courage to look at ourselves with greater honesty and compassion. Both must be aligned in each of us. And we must learn to serenely bear the pain of being displeasing to ourselves, or the process of self-discovery will continually elude us. Self-understanding, compassion, and humility are the internal counterparts of empathy and clarity in guiding others to be their best and are necessary conditions for the pursuit of excellence.

What Have We Learned?

- Humility can be thought of as knowing yourself as you truly are. Self-knowledge and hubris are not compatible.

- The optimal organization in the twenty-first century is the learning organization, an organization that discovers how to tap people's commitment and capacity to learn at all levels and that continually evolves its capacity to create its own future.

- Commitment to a relationship or an organization is a function of the possibility of growth.

- In systems thinking, every influence is both cause and effect; we all contribute and influence our reality on a relatively continuous basis.

- Cultural change in organizations requires a self-aware leader who is focused on addressing limits on growth in his or her company.

- The most effective way of furthering self-discovery and self-knowledge in a business context is probably through expert coaching.

- Self-understanding, compassion, and humility are the internal counterparts of empathy and clarity in guiding others to be their best and are necessary conditions for the pursuit of excellence.

The Hall of Mirrors: Looking at Ourselves

Developing the qualities associated with greatness starts with changing self-limiting beliefs. Begin by keeping your biggest dreams in your consciousness. Doing this can stimulate the creation of new pathways and connections in the brain. Being open to a greater life starts with one step. There are some specific actions you can take to begin the process of achieving greater clarity about yourself and others.

EI [emotional intelligence] leadership...builds up from a foundation of self-awareness.

Goleman, Boyatzis, & McKee, 2002

We should not pretend to understand the world only by the intellect; we apprehend it just as much by feeling. Therefore, the judgment of the intellect is, at best, only the half of truth, and must, if it be honest, also come to an understanding of its inadequacy.

Carl Jung, 1921

I learned some important things about myself as a leader and honed my skill sets over time. But some of this was really small-circle achievement. Hence, the satisfaction associated with new accomplishments was relatively short-lived. I felt as though I had to earn my wings every day, a belief that required me to attend to everything, sometimes at the expense of more important things. I later realized that this was a symptom of small-circle achievement, a type of achievement that influences what we present on the outside in a way that validates our self-limiting, tacit, internal mental models. When we confine ourselves to small-circle achievement, we tend to define ourselves too narrowly and fail to take fuller advantage of our unrealized potential. We may meet others' expectations, but we know that more of us could be put to meaningful use. In this state, relative success becomes confused with genuine personal mastery, which requires us to change our mental models. Often the intensity of our drive and sense of urgency associated with tasks and responsibilities are energized by forces that have little to do with excellence. The unraveling of my unconscious illusions of immunity from illness and disappointment began at mid-life. It was the start of a painful but productive process that, like my earlier relaxation tape experience, reminded me that I still had a great deal to learn about myself. Like my father's wisely chosen gift, I could not have anticipated it and could not push it away. It required that I question everything—and I did. My self-curiosity led me to pursue psychoanalytic studies that complemented my previous research-based academic pursuits in clinical psychology. I completed many years of coursework, training analysis, presentations, reports, and examinations and received my psychoanalytic certificate in 2010.

Although I gained a totally different perspective on human development and functioning than that provided by my traditional academic training, the most important learning I did during this period resulted from the training analysis itself, which taught me about how my own mind worked and the basis for many of my actions and beliefs. As my awareness increased, I began to notice that many things were slowly changing in my life. I saw other people differently and focused on them in a completely novel way. More important, they could sense this change, and, as a consequence, my effectiveness as a leader, executive coach, and a person was transformed. Another welcome result? I felt less driven but was able to accomplish much more in the same amount of time. I noticed that calm energy had replaced driven energy, and I often felt refreshed at the end of a long day—a feeling I'd rarely had before. I knew, for the first time in my life, the meaning of Whyte's "all things change when we do."

Sometimes when we are ready the right experience presents itself. During the time that our university think tank was meeting on a regular basis, I had the good fortune to read Cooper's *The Other 90%* (2001b). Before I even got to chapter 1, I read two statements that confirmed what I had sensed all along: "studies indicate that we use not one-tenth but *one ten-thousandth* of our capabilities" (p. xvi) and "the next frontier is not only in front of you, it is inside you" (p. xvii). The idea that nerve, trust, energy, and farsightedness were the keys to unlocking potential helped me to look at my experience as a leader from a new and promising vantage point.

This chapter is designed to help you move beyond understanding to self-discovery. Four illustrations in the form of "mirrors" will demonstrate how empirically supported ideas derived from history, psychology, neuroscience, and organizational effectiveness relate to each other and how they can be applied to you and your organization. Historical wisdom learned from studying the essential qualities of great leaders is likely to be recognized and embraced by most cultures throughout our globally interconnected world. Although science and technology have created abundant knowledge of our potential for change, many still believe that its application is limited by human nature. New findings in the fields of neuroscience and psychology are shedding light on why human nature appears to have remained unchanged throughout history and demonstrating how our unrealized potential can be liberated and converted into kinetic energy. Designing organizations that are capable of learning, changing, and innovating is within our reach. We now understand how to develop learning organizations that can create visions of desired futures and enable us to recognize and appreciate the value of our interdependence, energizing us to know ourselves, improve ourselves, and cooperate with one another.

Recall that J. Rufus Fears (2007) identified (a) a bedrock of principles, (b) a moral compass, (c) a vision, and (d) the ability to build a consensus to achieve that vision as qualities of great leaders (i.e., statesmen as opposed to mere politicians). He also identified truth, wisdom, justice, courage, and moderation as values of those who led great civilizations across place, time, and culture. (Hubris, considered the fundamental sin, was described simply as the abuse of the weak by the powerful.) Fears' great contribution to our field, *The Wisdom of History*, demonstrates the enduring nature of these qualities in civilizations that thrived for years.

Here we have updated the definitions of these leadership values as they relate to our purpose, and added a sixth, trust, to the list.[8]

> **Truth**: Fidelity to a standard of honesty, integrity, and sincerity, reflecting humility achieved through the acquisition of self-knowledge.

> **Wisdom**: The use of astute judgment guided by a bedrock of principles, a moral compass, and high aspirations and ideals for yourself and others in putting knowledge to use.

> **Justice**: Moral rightness in action and attitude guided by a commitment to treat others as we would like to be treated.

> **Courage**: The confidence to act in accordance with one's beliefs when a course of action involves danger, fear, or pain and is more difficult to pursue than other courses of action.

---

[8] Trust was added to the list since it represented a keystone in Cooper's *The Other 90%* (2001b). Several of these ideas for unlocking untapped potential come from his works on the neuroscience of leadership.

Moderation: Sustaining optimal levels of performance by maintaining moderate drive and energy levels for extended periods of time.

Trust: Believing in the unproven integrity, ability, and character of another person or experience based on confidence energized by a high level of self-worth and realistic self-knowledge.

While highly valued, commitment to truth and justice seem to be closely associated with moral development and may actually result from honing and internalizing the remaining characteristics on the list. One thing is clear—the value and importance assigned to these characteristics tend to increase with self-knowledge. Individuals in whom a sense of truth and justice is significantly underdeveloped might best be advised to seek guidance from a psychologist coach or therapist licensed and credentialed to provide human services in this area. They can often help individuals learn how their mind works and how psychological defenses can keep them from knowing themselves as they truly are. Over time, it is possible for these individuals to see the essential value of honesty and fairness as a framework for working with him- or herself and others. The realization that there is no rule of conduct that exceeds simple sincerity and honesty is a product of maturity and self-knowledge.

Here, we will explore the remaining four characteristics—wisdom, courage, moderation, trust—as they relate to the use of power and freedom in twenty-first-century work environments. In this respect, it is important to note Fears' observation (2007) that "great nations [companies] rise and fall because of human decisions, not anonymous social and economic forces." We expand on his belief that history has important lessons to teach individuals and groups to include companies as well as nations. Decisions made by those at the top have the broadest impact on a company's or an industry's future success. These principles hold true for all systems, from small emerging companies to large, complex, multinational organizations.

Creating consensus in organizations is largely influenced by leadership self-knowledge, empathy, interpersonal connectedness, and a capacity to inspire voluntary enrollment in the service of meaningful ideas. I have seen the benefits to companies and organizations from the application of these qualities in my own work with CEOs and in organizations.

We'll examine each of the four characteristics by looking into a "mirror"—a reflection of how we see ourselves today—and asking some essential questions. Our assessment and subsequent recommendations align closely with the ideas of two highly respected authors who approach personal and organizational effectiveness from very different perspectives. First, they directly address the keystones that Cooper (2001b) touts as essential in recapturing our untapped potential. Second, they conform closely to the five disciplines that must be mastered to create a learning organization, as delineated in Senge's *The Fifth Discipline* (2006). I encourage the reader to examine these works for a more in-depth treatment of the considerations and insights offered in this chapter.

Wisdom

Look into the mirror and ask yourself, "Are all customer, management, and employee transactions and interactions thoughtfully guided by the company's shared vision and the highest aspirations for all constituencies?"

If your answer to this question is "yes," congratulations! You understand the value of knowing what's important to employees and the benefit of their full participation in the creation of the company's vision and strategic planning. You recognize that commitment is a function of the potential for growth in a context in which the needs of customers, employees, and management are illuminated and highly valued.

If you could not confidently answer "yes" or answered "no," here are some insights that can help change your answer.

Keep your eye on the big picture.
- Your biggest dreams will awaken your heart. Make sure that your reach exceeds your grasp.

- Establish a "long-term time horizon"—it will put your life into perspective and help you to know yourself better now.

- Develop a habit of doing the "harder thing." If you do this with regularity, you'll engage the prefrontal areas of your brain, which have the capacity to override the amygdale, the sometimes over-reactive "fear center" of the brain.

Incorporate several "wise actions" into your routine.
- Pause several times a day, and align your actions with the insights born of these pauses.

- Face difficult situations sooner rather than later.

- Exercise on a regular basis and be mindful of maintaining good nutrition in your diet. Both contribute to relaxed energy and clear thinking.

- Engage in play and laughter every day. Children do this naturally, and laughter contributes to good health.

- Don't take things too seriously. After calm reflection, there are few things that cannot be fixed or improved.

- Change before you have to—it is a mark of a great leader. It is actually safer than changing when you have to (a mark of a good leader).

Maintain an enlightened perspective.
- Look at an issue from several sides—it will look different from each vantage point.

- Accept the parts of yourself you consider unlikeable with serenity.

- Cultivate a "beginner's mind" by looking at familiar things in a different way.

- Don't take yourself too seriously.

- Keep your will steadfastly toward the good. Often, things that come to us too easily gratify us for the moment but leave us as we were before.

- Learn what effective leaders know. Emotions constitute the language of leadership.

Courage
Look into the mirror and ask yourself, "Are all constituencies in my organization encouraged to be curious about how they limit access to their greater potential and to dream about what they could offer themselves and the organization if they reach beyond what they think is possible?"

If your answer to this question is "yes," congratulations! You understand that a commitment to personal mastery requires courage and is an indispensable ingredient in creating new knowledge through excellence. An organization that recognizes this enjoys a competitive advantage over those that pursue linear change.

If you could not confidently answer "yes" or answered "no," here are some insights that can help change your answer.

Resist equating ambiguity with danger; instead, be curious about possibilities.
- Learn that clarity follows involvement and reasonable risks.

- Stay open to the unknown in yourself, and life will present you with defining moments that offer a glimpse at your future life.

- Look straight ahead. The best way out of difficulty is through it.

- Don't confuse self-doubt with other types of fear. We sometimes fear expanding the image of our potential more than we fear failure.

- Remember that it may be most dangerous to avoid all risks in life.

Maintain steadfastness.
- Never abandon your truth, known only to your heart.

- Say "yes" to your higher destiny; greater clarity will emerge.

- Don't use gradualness as a way of avoiding action that creates change.

- Learn to calmly bear the pain of being displeasing to yourself.

- Genuinely care for others—it nourishes your soul.

Know what it means to act courageously.
- When faced with adversity, don't add to it. Engage in positive distractions that require no course of action.

- When you don't know what to do, do a lot of different things.

- Act with simple sincerity and honesty—there is no rule of conduct that has more power than this.

- Embrace the adventure of life by breaking new ground whenever you can.

- Work at becoming your complete self, and contemplate your unique legacy to the world.

- Attend to your gut, heart, and head before taking action.

Look at adversity in a different way.
- Learn the difference between resistance to change and real danger.

- Do not fear adversity. Many important lessons are learned when you endure what you thought was unendurable and accomplish what you thought was impossible.

- Broaden your options by decoupling current challenges from past adversity.

- Accept your plight as a gift rather than as an unfair burden.

- Learn to tolerate the anxiety associated with uncertainty and change.

- Develop a precarious view of your own certainty, especially when faced with adversity.

- Avoid "magical thinking" in the face of ambiguity. In the absence of hard evidence, allow yourself to "not know."

Moderation

Look in the mirror and ask yourself, "Do employees in my company consistently create high quality outcomes in an effective and streamlined manner, energized by curiosity, inner calmness, relaxed alertness, optimism, and a sense of well-being, sometimes referred to as *flow*?"

If your answer to this question is "yes," congratulations! You understand that optimal levels of performance are the result of intermediate or moderate levels of drive. You know the difference between tense energy and calm energy—and the unintended consequences of the former. You've learned how to tap into positive energy by helping high contributors in your company maintain internal harmony.

If you could not confidently answer "yes" or answered "no," here are some insights that can help change your answer.

Pace yourself.
- Take a long-term point of view. It will help you to see and consider more options.

- Get adequate sleep and rest.

- Begin your day calmly upon waking and move at a relaxed pace.

- Take pauses throughout the workday to enhance the speed and quality of your work.[9]

Maintain an attitude of relaxed engagement.
- Keep your priorities at the center of your actions and your focus on what is most important.

- Don't let minor disruptions divert your focus and energy from giving your very best.

- Find a way to incorporate humor throughout each day—it will help you broaden your perspective.

Work toward balance.
- Enjoy pleasurable experiences every day. They usually require frontal lobe participation.

- Spend more time developing your strengths and less time managing your weaknesses.

- Don't allow your focus to narrow so much that you overlook your broader life—family, friends, and meaningful causes.

Stay close to your heart and gut.
- Listen to your body. The language of the body often bypasses the censors in the brain.

- Stay in touch with your emotions. Emotions add value to the information

---

[9] Cooper (2001b) suggests that the following can improve accomplishment during pauses: deep and relaxed breathing, increased brightness, movement, sipping water (ice water helps burn calories), engaging in humor and lightheartedness, and keeping your larger purpose in mind.

generated by your intellect.

- Make sure that your work is aligned with your passions.

- Never ignore what you love; in fact, make it the center of your life.

- Learn about and own your unique gifts and offer them to the world.

- Look inside yourself for meaningful direction.

- Be realistic, but be more skeptical of negative messages than positive ones.

- Understand that accountability stems from the heart; it is the external expression of conscience.

Trust

Look into the mirror and ask yourself, "Are employees in my company aligned with the vision, energized by team participation, and willing to put forward innovative ideas and creative solutions that contribute to enhanced effectiveness?"

If your answer to this question is "yes," congratulations! You are an outstanding leader who has a *feel* for what matters; you live and lead using your gut, heart, and head. You know to make sure that your words reflect what you feel inside. You have learned that when people don't feel cared about and uniquely valued, they do not put their hearts into their life or their work.

If you could not confidently answer "yes" or answered "no," here are some insights that can help change your answer.

Develop empathy for others; it builds trust.
- Approach others with an open mind and an open heart.

- Don't make assumptions about others' motives; they are usually incorrect.

- Deal with others by "peeling the onion": Layer by layer, help one another understand what's driving the other's behaviors and feelings.

- Give others the benefit of the doubt, including yourself. The more serene your relationship with yourself, the easier it is to trust others.

• Allow others a way out with dignity.

Make sure that your words and actions are consistent with what you feel.
• Don't withhold or distort information.

• Be aware that negative evaluations create enduring consequences.

• Understand that mistrust compromises the quality and quantity of employees' work time.

• Realize that punishment suppresses the behavior of others, but does not eliminate it.

Focus on excellence over competition.
• Write down your most important values. Refer back to them frequently.

• Realize that pursuing excellence reduces the gap between actual functioning and functioning capacity.

• Understand that excellence is pursuing your best, not besting others; aspiration is reaching beyond your best.

• Don't compare yourself with others.

Strengthen your connections with others by initiating and affirming trust.
• Honor and value others' greatness.

• Be aware of what others care about; particularly, what excites them and consumes their energy.

• Engage in open dialogue with trusted others to reveal your own tacit mental models to yourself.

• Seek feedback from trusted others regarding their perception of your values.

• Listen to others with full engagement.

The value of self-knowledge

Self-knowledge influences the delivery system for everything you attempt in life. It is acquired by questioning what you know about yourself and preserving the parts that represent your true self. How objectively you see what is on the outside depends on how well you know what is on the inside. True self-knowledge requires us to transform from who we think we are to who we truly are, but hubris keeps us from looking too closely and enables us to settle for relative success in our lives and our work. The benefits of objective self-knowledge—including renewed energy in both ourselves and others—are tangible. Those who successfully achieve self-knowledge also tend to execute well. For them, outside feedback can be a good measure of actual achievement.

In this chapter, we have offered some suggestions that might help you more easily access your fuller potential. CEOeffectiveness.com presents some additional guidelines to consider on your journey. These recommendations may help you become aware of the blind spots that could keep you from accessing your greater potential. For those who desire the benefit of a professional guide, a few accomplished business consultants and coaches also may be accessed through the site.

Afterword

This book was designed to present information that is essential to the acquisition of self-knowledge, a prerequisite to personal mastery and organizational effectiveness in the twenty-first century. It presents essential ideas and resources and identifies next steps for CEOs and top leaders who are committed to their own personal mastery and that of their business or organization. It is possible to gain self-knowledge by learning from successes and mistakes, and how we interpret these experiences and execute change based on them is critical. Improvement can be achieved by looking through the metaphorical lenses calibrated by the mental models of the past, but the rapture of full engagement in life and work will always elude us.

Top business leaders are an indispensable part of the systems that drive the success of their companies and organizations. Their execution of change is influenced by the objectivity and clarity of their self-knowledge. In this book we have looked at the works of great thinkers whose knowledge base was constructed from decades of research. The manner in which these great ideas are implemented makes a huge difference to the bottom line. We can all learn something from spouses, friends, colleagues, and employees. But even when they offer us their very best, a selection bias remains in operation since their mental models tend to resonate with ours. That's why we trust them and, in the cases of our friends and employees, that's why we picked them.

The paradox of self-knowledge is that it is best acquired interpersonally. But if we can't accomplish this alone, and if trusted others are not able to stretch us enough to change our mental models—in spite of their best intentions—how can we ever reduce the gap between our functioning level and our capability?

This book is the beginning of a journey that begins with knowledge and leads to understanding and self-discovery. Wherever you might be on your journey, the ideas presented herein will help you evolve your capacity to create the outcomes you desire.

References and Additional Reading

The Arbinger Institute. (2000). *Leadership and self-deception: Getting out of the box*. San Francisco, CA: Berrett-Koehler.

Cooper, R. K. (2001a). *The neuroscience of leadership*. Workshop presented in Tampa, FL.

Cooper, R. K. (2001b). *The other 90%: How to unlock your vast untapped potential for leadership and life*. New York, NY: Three Rivers Press.

Cooper, R. K. (2006). *Get out of your own way: The 5 keys to surpassing everyone's expectations*. New York, NY: Crown Business.

Covey, S. R. (1989). *The 7 habits of highly effective people*. New York, NY: Simon and Schuster.

Doidge, N. (2007). *The brain that changes itself: Stories of personal triumph from the frontiers of brain science*. New York, NY: Penguin.

Einstein, A. (1946). Atomic education urged by Einstein. *New York Times*, May 25, 13.

Einstein, A. (1950, February 12). *Letter to Robert S. Marcus, Albert Einstein Archives*. Retrieved from http://blog.onbeing.org/post/241572419/einstein-sleuthing-by-nancy-rosenbaum-associate.

Eliot, T. S. (1943). *Four quartets*. Orlando, FL: Harcourt.

Fears, J. R. (2007). *The wisdom of history* [audio recording]. Chantilly, VA: The Teaching Company.

Godin, S. (2012, May 24). *If I were you* [blog entry]. Retrieved from http://sethgodin.typepad.com/.

Goleman, D. (2005). *Emotional intelligence*. New York, NY: Bantam Dell.

Goleman, D. (2007, August 3). *Authors@Google: Daniel Goleman* [video recording]. Retrieved from http://www.youtube.com/watch?v=-hoo_dIOP8k&feature=player_embedded.

Goleman, D., Boyatzis, R., & McKee, A. (2002). *Primal leadership: Realizing the power of emotional intelligence.* Boston, MA: Harvard Business School Press.

Jung, C. G. (1921). *Psychologische typen [Psychological types].* Zurich, Switzerland: Rascher Verlag.

Kirkpatrick, D. (2011, September 7). *Social power and the coming corporate revolution: Why employees and customers will be calling the shots.* Retrieved from www.forbes.com.

Lencioni, P. M. (2012). *The advantage: Why organizational health trumps everything else in business.* San Francisco, CA: Jossey-Bass.

Lieberman, D. J. (1997). *Instant analysis.* New York, NY: St. Martin's Press.

Morris, E. (2005). *Beethoven: The universal composer (eminent lives).* New York, NY: Harper Collins.

Peck, M. S. (1985). *The road less traveled: A new psychology of love, traditional values, and spiritual growth.* New York, NY: Simon and Schuster.

Peck, M. S. (1993). *A world waiting to be born: Civility rediscovered.* New York, NY: Bantam Books.

Pert, C. B. (1999). *Molecules of emotion: The science behind mind-body medicine.* New York, NY: Touchstone.

Pert, C. B. (2004). *Your body is your subconscious mind* [audio CD]. Louisville, CO: Sounds True.

Senge, P. M. (2006). *The fifth discipline: The art and practice of the learning organization (rev. ed.).* New York, NY: Doubleday.

Shenk, D. (2011). *The genius in all of us: New insights into genetics, talent, and IQ.* New York, NY: Anchor Books.

Smith, J. L. (2006). *Creating competitive advantage*. New York, NY: Crown Publishing.

Varey, W. (2009, June 24). *Einstein enigmatic quote* [blog entry]. Retrieved from http://icarus-falling.blogspot.com/.

Whyte, D. (2002). *The heart aroused: Poetry and the preservation of the soul in corporate America (rev. ed.)*. New York, NY: Doubleday.

Williamson, M. (1992). *A return to love: Reflections on the principles of 'A course in miracles.'* New York, NY: Harper Collins.

Yerkes, R. M., & Dodson, J. D. (1908). The relation of strength of stimulus to rapidity of habit-formation. *Journal of Comparative Neurology and Psychology, 18*, 459-482.

Appendix A
Daily Activities to Increase Self-Knowledge

Here we list some things leaders can do to begin increasing their self-knowledge. For an updated list, refer to www.ceoeffectiveness.com.

Meditation. This appears to allow more information to reach the frontal cortex and enables us to discard some of the noise that keeps us from seeing reality.

Prayer. With some of the benefits of meditation, prayer allows freer access to the center of our being, which may be located in the frontal cortex.

Self-discipline (i.e., doing the harder thing). This habit often leads to disconfirming experiences that disrupt habitual pathways to the frontal cortex, gradually allowing possibilities to override stagnating habits.

Not judging. This allows more real information to get to the frontal lobes. Gather information from others. List the things you find intolerable in others and ask trusted persons if they see any of those attributes in you.

Remind yourself that ambiguity is not equivalent to danger. Learn to tolerate anxiety without taking impulsive action to reduce your discomfort. (Social-evaluative anxiety is often a sign that we have enough cortical matter to be faced with choices and is usually reduced once a realistic direction is identified.)

Be skeptical of your assumptions. Ask others what they think and listen to them with a "beginner's mind." As you begin to question your own certainty, your mind becomes more receptive to improved quality in your own life.

Engage in self-talk that disconfirms your assumptions. The quality of this self-talk should improve significantly if you are engaging in some of the other suggestions on this list.

Change habitual ways of dealing with high levels of stress. This helps to override hardwired brain tendencies. Talking things out with trusted others can be very helpful.

Take a long-term perspective. Long-term self-interest creates better results than short-term self-interest since the consequences of our actions are often experienced remotely in time.

Think about the perspective of your direct reports. Work at putting yourself in others' shoes. It can reveal your tacit mental models.

Appendix B
Image Descriptions

External guides can be relied on only until they are embedded in our brain circuitry and we are able to lead from the heart.

Early mental models are often perpetuated simply because we don't know they exist.

Pursuing excellence requires that you commit to reducing the gap between tacit mental models established early in life and your unrealized potential.

Great leaders are guided by a moral compass and achieve remarkable outcomes by pursuing truth, wisdom, justice, courage, and moderation.

Hubris keeps us from knowing ourselves as we truly are and limits the quality of the feedback we receive from others.

Early perceptions and beliefs tend to solidify and strengthen as we grow older because we contribute to what we see.

Engaging your prefrontal lobes when listening connects you to others through meaning and minimizes resistance.

Helping others grow and become more effective increases their commitment to the leader and to the organization.

Optimal levels of performance are achieved at intermediate levels of arousal. Too little or too much arousal or drive is associated with weaker performance levels. Extreme levels of drive or arousal can result in negative physiological consequences or, in the extreme, impairment.

Knowing how our mind works aligns our perceptions and accompanying actions with reality.

Productive energy is liberated through alignment of purpose.

If we can't see who we are, it is not possible to know others and much more difficult to inspire followership.